**Cambridge Primary**

# Hodder Cambridge Primary

# Maths

## Learner's Book

## Stage 1

## Paul Wrangles

**Series editors: Mike Askew and Paul Broadbent**

**HODDER EDUCATION**
AN HACHETTE UK COMPANY

With warm thanks to Jan Fisher for her help in shaping and developing this title.

The Publisher is extremely grateful to the following schools for their comments and feedback during the development of this series:

Avalon Heights World Private School, Ajman

The Oxford School, Dubai

Al Amana Private School, Sharjah

British International School, Ajman

Wesgreen International School, Sharjah

As Seeb International School, Al Khoud.

Every effort has been made to trace all copyright holders, but if any have been inadvertently overlooked the Publishers will be pleased to make the necessary arrangements at the first opportunity.

**Photograph acknowledgements**

We would like to thank the following for their permission to reproduce photographs:

**p.21, p.32 (all), p.50 (all), p.51 (all), p.56 (both), p.65 (all), p.104 (all), p.105 (all); p.130 (both)** © Hachette UK; **p.40** © Chris Putnam/123rf; **p.41** © Kunpisit Riawklang/123rf; **p.46** © C Squared Studios/Getty Images; **p.54** t © Eden Breitz/Alamy Stock Photo; **p.54** cl © Oksana Kuzmina/Shutterstock; **p.54** bl © Stock Connection Blue/Alamy Stock Photo; **p.54** c © Jovannig/123rf;

**p.54** tr © Stock Connection Blue/Alamy Stock Photo; **p.54** cr © Africa Media Online/Alamy Stock Photo;

**p.54** br © Inspirestock International/123rf; **p.55** tl © Zerbor123rf; **p.55** tr © Ruslan Grigolava/123rf; p.131tl © Monticello/Shutterstock; **p.131** tr © Turtix/Shutterstock

t = top, b = bottom, l = left, r = right, c = centre

Although every effort has been made to ensure that website addresses are correct at time of going to press, Hodder Education cannot be held responsible for the content of any website mentioned in this book. It is sometimes possible to find a relocated web page by typing in the address of the home page for a website in the URL window of your browser.

Hachette UK's policy is to use papers that are natural, renewable and recyclable products and made from wood grown in sustainable forests. The logging and manufacturing processes are expected to conform to the environmental regulations of the country of origin.

Orders: please contact Bookpoint Ltd, 130 Milton Park, Abingdon, Oxon OX14 4SB. Telephone: (44) 01235 827720. Fax: (44) 01235 400454. Lines are open from 9.00–5.00, Monday to Saturday, with a 24 hour message answering service. You can also order through our website www.hoddereducation.com

© Paul Wrangles 2017

Published by Hodder Education

An Hachette UK Company

Carmelite House, 50 Victoria Embankment, London EC4Y 0DZ

Impression number    5 4 3

Year                 2021  2020  2019  2018

Cover illustration by Steve Evans

Illustrations by Jeanne du Plessis, Vian Oelofsen and Steve Evans

Typeset in FS Albert 17 on 19pt by IO Publishing CC

Printed in India

A catalogue record for this title is available from the British Library

9781471884313

# Contents

I am Maya.

I am Lev.

# Introduction

**Explore** the picture or problem.

What do you see?

What can you find?

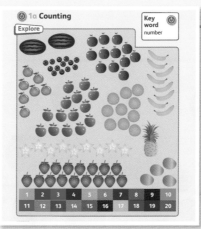

**Key words** are in a list for you to learn.

**Learn** new maths skills with your teacher. Look at the pictures to help you.

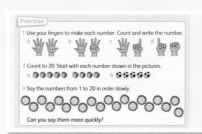

**Practise** the maths you have learnt. Write any answers in your exercise book.

**Try this** challenge activity to make you think carefully about the maths.

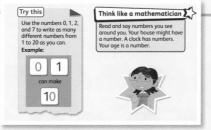

Read these hints and tips to help you **think like a mathematician**.

At the end of each unit try the **self-check** activities. What have you learnt?

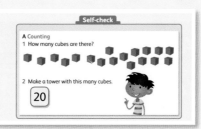

# Unit 1 Number and problem solving

## 1a Counting

**Explore**

| 1 | 2 | 3 | 4 | 5 | 6 | 7 | 8 | 9 | 10 |
|---|---|---|---|---|---|---|---|---|---|
| 11 | 12 | 13 | 14 | 15 | 16 | 17 | 18 | 19 | 20 |

## Saying numbers in order

### Learn

Say these numbers in order.
Put your finger on each number as you say it.

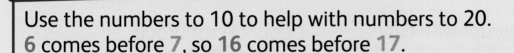

| 1 | 2 | 3 | 4 | 5 | 6 | 7 | 8 | 9 | 10 |
| 11 | 12 | 13 | 14 | 15 | 16 | 17 | 18 | 19 | 20 |

### Think like a mathematician

Use the numbers to 10 to help with numbers to 20.
6 comes before 7, so 16 comes before 17.

### Practise

1 Use your fingers to make each number. Count and write the number.

a    b   c   d

2 Count to 20. Start with each number shown in the pictures.

a    b

3 Say the numbers from 1 to 20 in order slowly.

Can you say them more quickly?

## Counting up to 20 objects

### Learn

How many balls are there?

Point to each ball. Say each number to count them.

1 2 3 4 5    6 7 8 9 10    11 12 13 14

There are 14 balls.

### Practise

1 Make these groups with cubes.

a

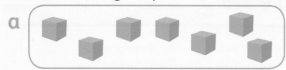

I used ___ cubes.

b

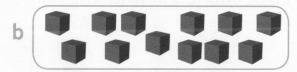

I used ___ cubes.

c

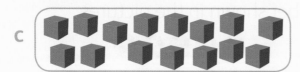

I used ___ cubes.

d

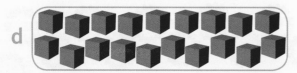

I used ___ cubes.

2 Count each group.

a

There are ___ circles.

b

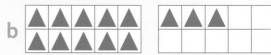

There are ___ triangles.

c

There are ___ squares.

d

There are ___ stars.

3 Count as you do these.

a Draw 8 circles.

b Make a pile of 10 books.

c Draw 17 triangles.

## Reading and writing numbers

**Learn**

Read the numbers from 1 to 20 in order.

1 2 3 4 5 6 7 8 9 10 11 12 13 14 15 16 17 18 19 20

**Practise**

1 Draw these numbers in the air with your finger.

a **12**   b **15**   c **18**   d **20**

2 Use your finger to trace each number. Say the number as you trace it.

| 1 | 2 | 3 | 4 | 5 |
|---|---|---|---|---|
| 6 | 7 | 8 | 9 | 10 |
| 11 | 12 | 13 | 14 | 15 |
| 16 | 17 | 18 | 19 | 20 |

**3** Use a number track to help you fill in the missing numbers.

a
| 1 | 2 | 3 | | 5 | 6 | | 8 | | 10 |
|---|---|---|---|---|---|---|---|---|---|

b
| 11 | 12 | 13 | | | 16 | 17 | 18 | | 20 |
|---|---|---|---|---|---|---|---|---|---|

c
| 5 | | 7 | | 9 | | 11 | | 13 | |
|---|---|---|---|---|---|---|---|---|---|

d
| 1 | 2 | | 4 | 5 | 6 | 7 | | 9 | 10 |
|---|---|---|---|---|---|---|---|---|---|

e
| 11 | | 13 | | 15 | | | 18 | | 20 |
|---|---|---|---|---|---|---|---|---|---|

**Try this**

Use the numbers 0, 1, 2, and 7 to write as many different numbers from 1 to 20 as you can.

**Example:**

**Think like a mathematician**

Read and say numbers you see around you. Your house might have a number. A clock has numbers. Your age is a number.

# 1b Comparing numbers

## Explore

Someone has mixed up these numbers!

3 7 2 1 4 9 10 6 5 8

15 17 12 13 14 19 18 16 11 20

What order should they be in?

## Bigger and smaller numbers

## Learn

Use tens frames to make each number.

12

15

Who has the bigger number?

## Practise

1 Use cubes to make pairs of towers. Which tower is taller?
The first one has been done for you.

a 9 cubes or 5 cubes?

The tower of
9 cubes is taller.

b 8 cubes or 10 cubes?

c 13 cubes or 14 cubes?

d 20 cubes or 19 cubes?

e 15 cubes or 5 cubes?

**2** Count each kind of shape. Which has more?

a

b

c

**3** Look at each pair of numbers. Which is bigger?

a ⭐7 ⭐8    b ⭐12 ⭐9    c ⭐13 ⭐19    d ⭐16 ⭐14

## Think like a mathematician

If you have two numbers and you are not sure which is more, look for the numbers on a number track and compare them.

## Putting numbers in order

**Learn**

**1** Order these numbers from smallest to largest.

16  17  15  14

**2** Write the smallest number first.

14  16  17  15

**3** Now write the next smallest number.

14  15  17  16

**4** What is the next smallest number?

14  15  16  17

These numbers are now in order from smallest to largest.

## Practise

1 Make towers of cubes.
  Order them from smallest to largest.

a
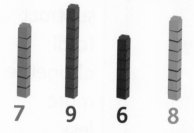

  7   9   6   8

b
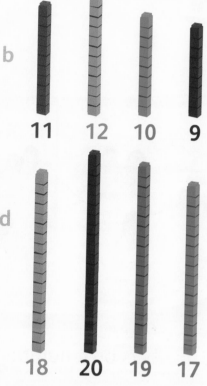

  11   12   10   9

c
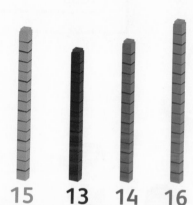

  15   13   14   16

d

  18   20   19   17

2 These number cards have not been pegged in the right order.
  Write them in the correct order.

a

  4   6   3   5

b

  8   10   7   9

c

  14   11   13   12

3 Write each set in order from smallest to largest.

a   6   1   13   9

b   15   8   3   11

c   12   10   14   17

d   19   15   8   20

### Try this

Put these numbers in two
different orders.

14  17  18  16  15

# 1c Addition and subtraction

**Explore**

**Key words**
add
take away
subtract
total
altogether
more
less

Make totals of 6 people in different ways.

Who is at 2 less than 7?

# Finding totals

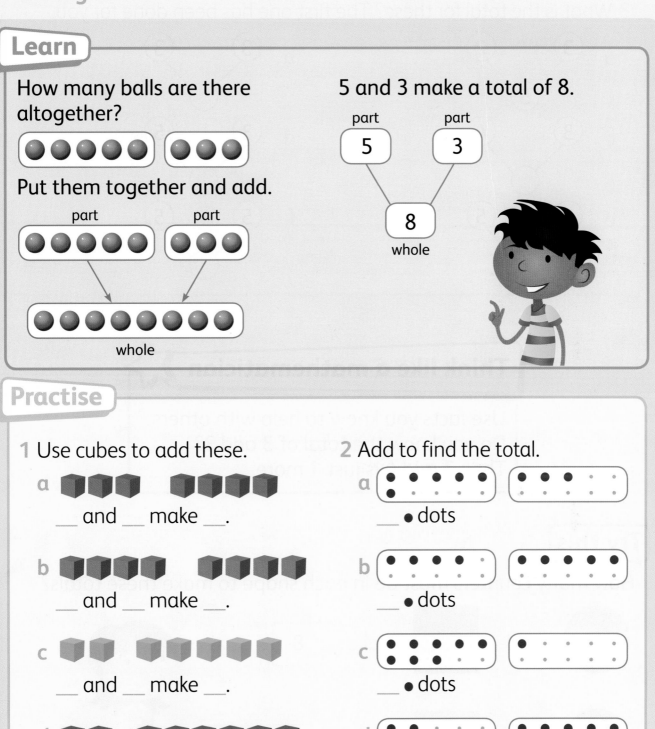

## Learn

How many balls are there altogether?

Put them together and add.

part          part

whole

5 and 3 make a total of 8.

part          part

5            3

8

whole

## Practise

1 Use cubes to add these.

a
__ and __ make __.

b
__ and __ make __.

c
__ and __ make __.

d
__ and __ make __.

2 Add to find the total.

a
__ dots

b
__ dots

c
__ dots

d
__ dots

15

3 What is the total for these? The first one has been done for you.

a  ③ — ② 
   ⑤

b  ③ — ③ 
   ○

c  ③ — ④ 
   ○

d  ③ — ⑤ 
   ○

e  ④ — ⑤ 
   ○

f  ⑤ — ⑤ 
   ○

## Think like a mathematician

Use facts you know to help with others.
Do you know the total of 3 add 3?
Then **3** add **4** is just **1** more.

## Try this

How many counters must be in each shape to make these totals?

 and  make  8 .

 and  make  10 .

# Taking away

## Learn

There are 5 pies on this plate.
Jo takes away 3 pies.

How many pies are left on the plate?

Take away 3 pies from 5 pies and 2 are left on the plate.

whole

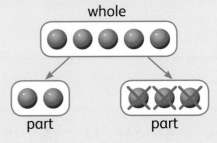

part          part

5 take away 3 leaves 2.

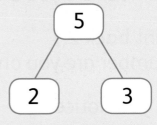

## Practise

1 Write the number sentence for these pictures.

a

6 take away __ leaves __.

b

5 take away __ leaves __.

c

7 take away __ leaves __.

d

8 take away __ leaves __.

**2** Use counters to help answer these.

a 7 take away 1 ⟶ _____

b 7 take away 3 ⟶ _____

c 7 take away 5 ⟶ _____

d 7 take away 7 ⟶ _____

**3** Write the missing number in each of these.

a
```
      5
     / \
    ○   3
```

b
```
      6
     / \
    ○   2
```

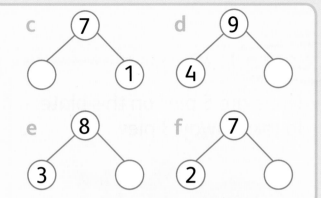

c
```
      7
     / \
    ○   1
```

d
```
      9
     / \
    4   ○
```

e
```
      8
     / \
    3   ○
```

f
```
      7
     / \
    2   ○
```

**Try this**

Write additions and subtractions for this picture.

## Counting on and back

**Learn**

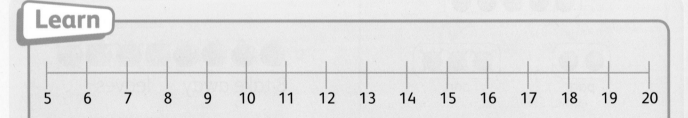

| 5 | 6 | 7 | 8 | 9 | 10 | 11 | 12 | 13 | 14 | 15 | 16 | 17 | 18 | 19 | 20 |

Put a finger on number 16.

Count **on** 1.
Which number are you on?

Now count **on** 2.
Which number are you on?

Now count **back** 1.
Which number are you on?

Now count **back** 2.
Which number are you on?

What do you notice?

**Practise**

1 Count on 2 for each of these. The first one has been done for you.

a **14 add 2 makes 16.**

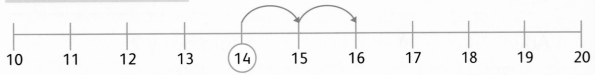

b 15 add 2 makes __.

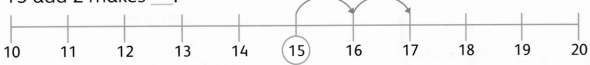

c 16 add 2 makes __.

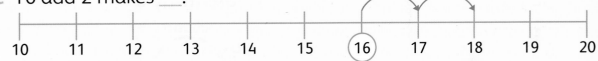

2 Count back 2 for each of these.

a 18 take away 2 leaves __.

b 17 take away 2 leaves __.

c 16 take away 2 leaves __.

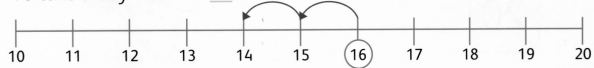

19

**3** Use a counter on this number track to help you add or subtract.

| 1 | 2 | 3 | 4 | 5 | 6 | 7 | 8 | 9 | 10 |
|---|---|---|---|---|---|---|---|---|----|

a Add 2

6 _____

b Add 3

6 _____

c Add 4

6 _____

d Take away 2

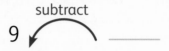
9 _____

e Take away 4

9 _____

f Take away 6

9 _____

## Self-check

**A** Counting

**1** How many cubes are there?

**2** Make a tower with this many cubes.

20

## B Comparing numbers

1 Which number is larger?

2 Put these number cards in order from smallest to largest.

## C Addition and subtraction

1 There are 10 cubes on this tray. How many cubes are under the other cup?

2 Write the missing number.

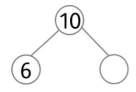

3 Copy this number line. Use it to show this addition.

6 add __ makes 10.

# Unit 2 Geometry and problem solving

## 2a Patterns and shapes

### Explore

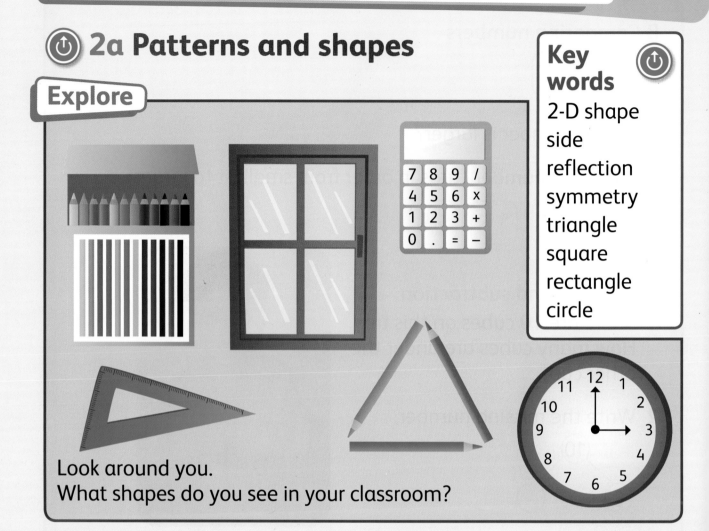

Look around you.
What shapes do you see in your classroom?

## Naming shapes

### Learn

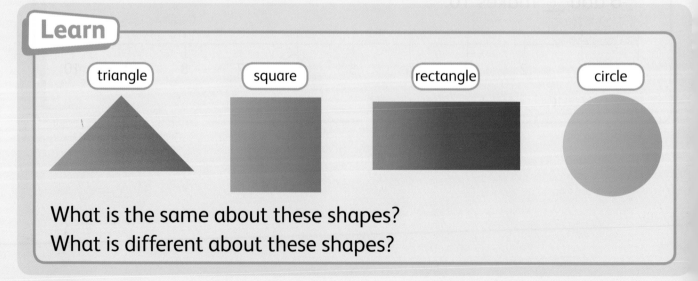

triangle    square    rectangle    circle

What is the same about these shapes?
What is different about these shapes?

## Practise

1 Match the shapes with the pictures.

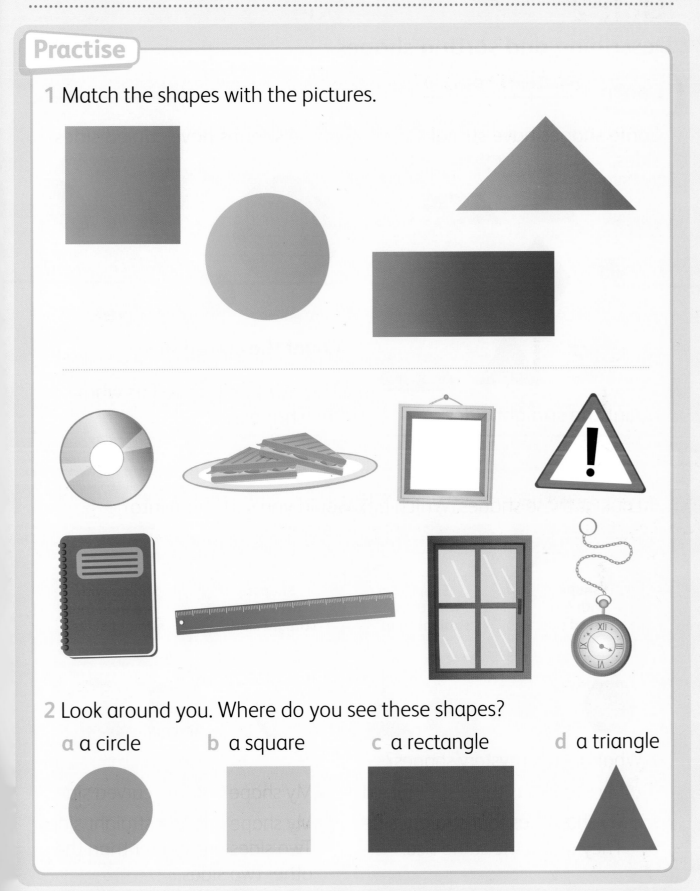

2 Look around you. Where do you see these shapes?

a a circle    b a square    c a rectangle    d a triangle

# Describing and sorting shapes

Some shapes have straight sides.

Count the straight sides.

Some shapes have curved sides.

Count the curved sides.

The sides help to tell us what the shape is.

**Practise**

1 Look at these shapes. Which box would you sort them into?

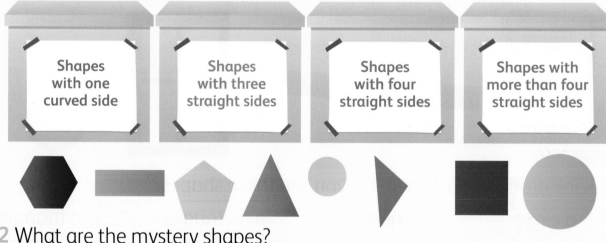

Shapes with one curved side

Shapes with three straight sides

Shapes with four straight sides

Shapes with more than four straight sides

2 What are the mystery shapes?

a My shape has three straight sides.

b My shape has one curved side.

c My shape has four straight sides. They are all the same size.

d My shape has four straight sides. Two sides are shorter than the other two sides.

# Making patterns and pictures

## Learn

We can make patterns or pictures by putting different shapes together.

This tree is made from a triangle and a rectangle.

Patterns repeat themselves.

This is repeated.

Which shape comes next?

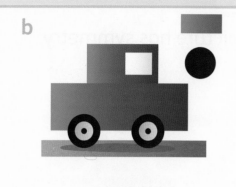

b

c

d

## Practise

1 Use shapes to draw each picture.

a

2 What comes next in each pattern?

a

b

c

# Reflections and symmetry

## Learn

This picture has symmetry.

This picture does not have symmetry.

Both halves of a picture with symmetry look the same.
Each half is a reflection of the other.

## Practise

Which of these shapes have symmetry?

1

2

3

4

## Try this

Find five different objects in your classroom that have symmetry.

Find five different objects in your classroom that do not have symmetry.

# 2b Making shapes

## Explore

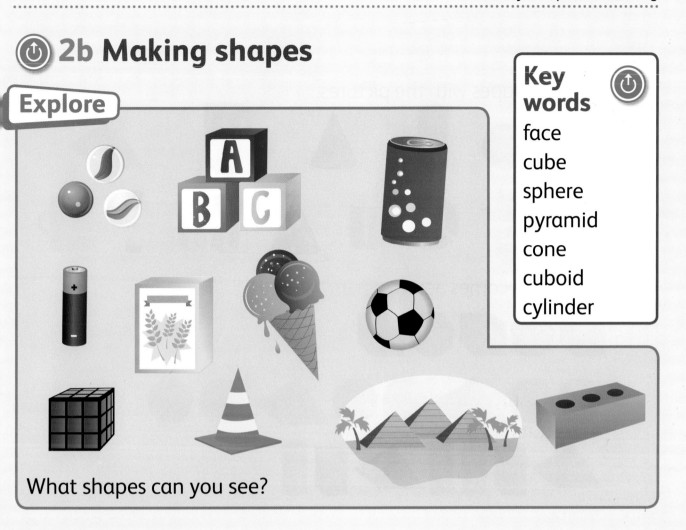

What shapes can you see?

## Naming shapes

### Learn

3-D shapes are solid shapes.

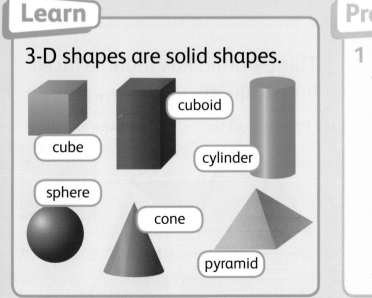

cuboid

cube

cylinder

sphere

cone

pyramid

### Practise

1 Make these 3-D shapes with clay.

a a cone

b a cube

c a sphere

d a pyramid

e a cuboid

f a cylinder

27

2 Match the shapes with the pictures.

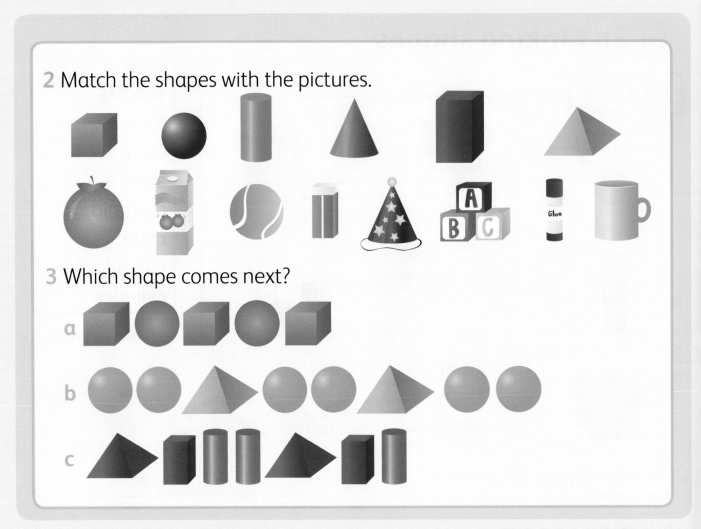

3 Which shape comes next?

a

b

c

## The faces of 3-D shapes

This cube has square faces.

This pyramid has triangle faces and a square face.

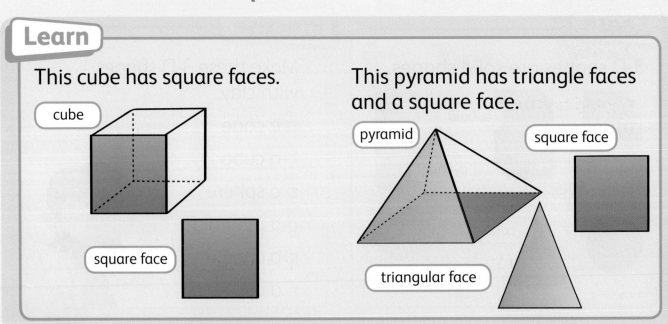

cube

square face

pyramid

square face

triangular face

This cylinder has a face that curves all the way around. There are circle faces at the top and bottom.

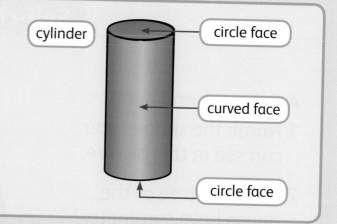

cylinder

circle face

curved face

circle face

## Practise

1 Press these 3-D shapes into clay or sand. What shapes do they make?

  a a cube   b a pyramid   c a cuboid   d the ends of a cylinder

2 Match these 3-D shapes with their faces.

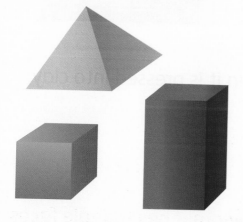

3 Khaled has written about the faces of some 3-D shapes. What are the 3-D shapes?

  a This shape has faces that are all squares.

  b This shape has rectangles and squares as its faces.

  c This shape has three triangles and one square face.

# Self-check

## A Patterns and shapes

1 Name the shapes you can see in this picture.

2 Does the tree or the house have symmetry?

3 How many shapes in the picture have straight sides?

4 How many shapes have curved sides?

## B Making shapes

This is the mark a 3-D shape makes when it is pressed into clay.

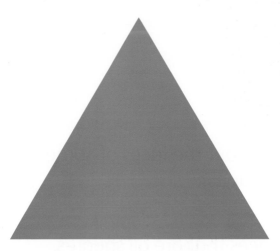

What could this shape be? Why?

# Unit 3 Number and problem solving

## ⏻ 3a Numbers to 20

**Explore**

What number is each animal on?

Start

1  2        7

12

Finish

15

18    20

How many birds are there?

**Key words** ⏻
how many
bigger
smaller

# Writing numbers

**Learn**

0   1   2   3   4   5   6   7   8   9

We can write all the numbers to 20 with these numbers.

**Practise**

1 Write these numbers in sand or rice using a stick.

a    b    c    d

2 Use your finger to trace each number onto the back of your hand.
   As you do it, say its name.

   What do you notice?

   a  1   2   3   4   5      b  6   7   8   9   10
      11 12 13 14 15            16 17 18 19 20

3 Write the two numbers that come after these.

   a 9 __ __      b 12 __ __      c 15 __ __      d 18 __ __

**Try this**

Write the numbers from 1 to 20.
How many numbers can you write without lifting your pencil off the page?

# How many are there?

We can count objects by pointing at them, touching them or moving them to one side.

How many are there?

How many are there now? Count to check. Are there more or less?

## Practise

**1** Count the numbers. Make them with cubes.

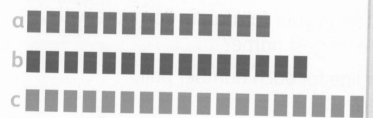

a

b

c

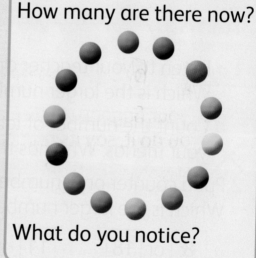

How many are there now?

What do you notice?

**2** How many are there?

a

b

**3** Try to find these objects in your classroom.

a 13 pencils    b 15 books    c 18 shoes

## Comparing numbers

**Learn**

Which number is more?

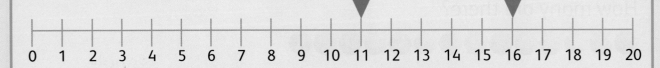

16 comes **after** 11, so **16** is **more** than **11**.

**Practise**

1 a Listen to your teacher clap and then tap a number of times. Which is the larger number?

b Count the number of letters in your full name. Compare with your friends. Who has the longest name?

2 Put a counter on a number line for each number pair. Which is the larger number?

a 8 or 18    b 11 or 9    c 16 or 12    d 17 or 19

3 Which number is the largest? How do you know?

a 8  2  5    b 6  13  10    c 12  15  20    d 17  19  18

**Try this**

Sofia and Sergio each take a number card.
Sofia says, "My number is 16."
Sergio says, "My number is bigger than yours and less than 20."
What could Sergio's number be?

# ⏱ 3b Addition and subtraction

**Key words**
add
take away
subtract
total
altogether
equals

## Explore

How can you make a group of 10?

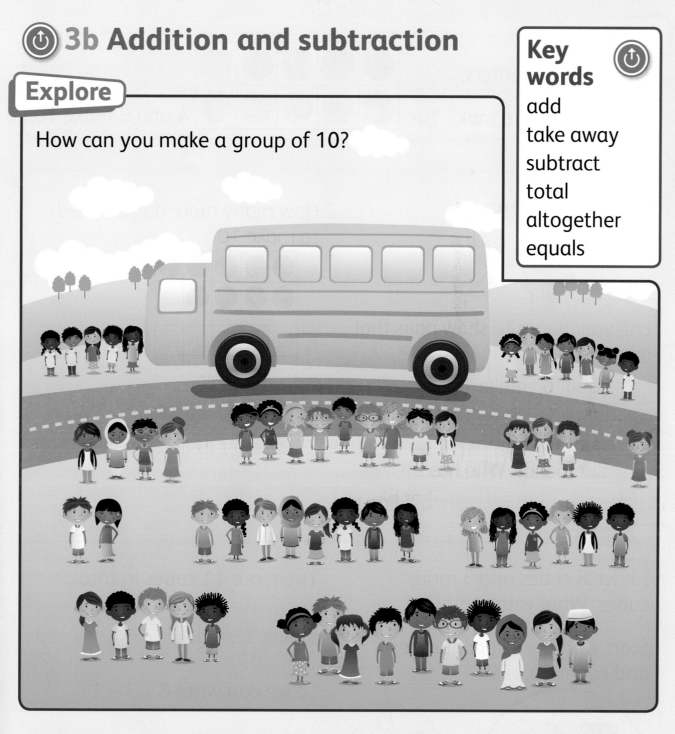

How many trips will the school bus make if only 10 children can go at a time?

Use the number line to help you make groups of 10.

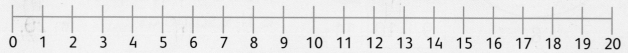

0  1  2  3  4  5  6  7  8  9  10  11  12  13  14  15  16  17  18  19  20

There are 4 counters.

How many more make 10?

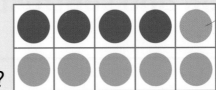

**4** and **6** make 10.

## Practise

**1** What makes 10?

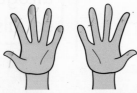

Use your hands to show pairs that make 10.

　a 5 and ⁵ make 10.

　b 8 and 2 make 10.

　c 3 and 7 make 10.

**2** How many more do you need to make 10?

a

b

c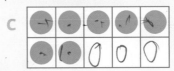

## Adding numbers by counting on

I have 8 cubes and 3 more cubes. What is the total?

Start with the larger number and count on.

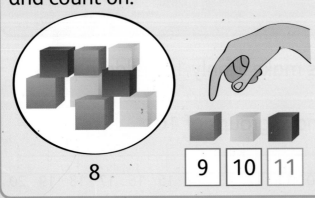

There are 11 cubes in total.

8 **plus** 3 **is equal to** 11.

So we can write 8 + 3 = 11

**+** means **plus**

**=** means **is equal to** or **is the same as**

## Practise

1 Use cubes. Count on to work out the total.

a 5 plus 3 equals ___ cubes.
b 7 plus 6 equals ___ cubes.

c 12 plus 5 equals ___ cubes.
d 9 plus 4 equals ___ cubes.

e 15 plus 2 equals ___ cubes.
f 11 plus 8 equals ___ cubes.

2 Count on to work out the total. The first one has been done for you.

a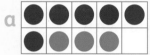

3 more than **6** is **9**.

b

5 more than 7 is ___.

c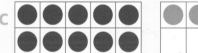

4 more than 10 is ___.

d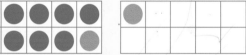

2 more than 9 is ___.

e

3 more than 8 is ___.

f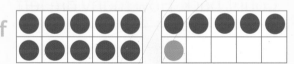

1 more than 15 is ___.

3 Use a number track to count on from the larger number.

| 1 | 2 | 3 | 4 | 5 | 6 | 7 | 8 | 9 | 10 |
|---|---|---|---|---|---|---|---|---|----|
| 11 | 12 | 13 | 14 | 15 | 16 | 17 | 18 | 19 | 20 |

a 5 + 4 = ___
b 5 + 9 = ___

c 4 + 12 = ___
d 13 + 6 = ___

e 18 + 2 = ___
f 5 + 15 = ___

# Subtracting numbers by counting back

**Learn**

If you have 9 cubes and take away 3, how many are left?

Count back from the first number.

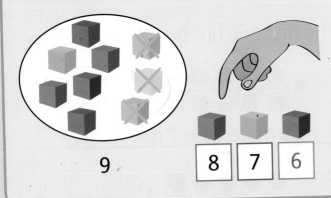

9

8 7 6

There are 6 cubes left.

9 take away 3 is equal to 6.

So we can write 9 − 3 = 6

− means **take away**

= means **is equal to** or **is the same as**

**Practise**

1 Count back. How many are left?

a

7

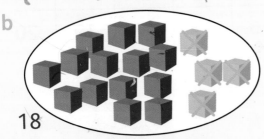

7 take away 3 equals 4.

b

18

18 take away 4 equals 14.

2 Count back on the tens frames.

a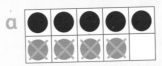

4 less than 9 is 5.

b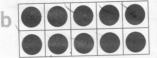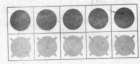

5 less than 20 is 15.

3 Use a number track. Count back from the first number.

a 10 − 5 = 5    b 13 − 3 = 15

c 19 − 4 = 15    d 14 − 7 = 7

## Solving problems

**Learn**

Do you need to add or take away to solve these problems?

Krishna has 16 nuts. She gives 4 to a friend. How many nuts does she have left?

Alisha has 16 nuts. She is given another 4. How many nuts does she have altogether?

**Practise**

1 Add or take away to find the answers.

  a There are 12 goats in a field. 5 of them escape. How many goats are left?

  b 4 children are sitting around a table. Another 3 children join them. How many children are sitting around the table now?

2 Count on or back to answer these.

  a There are 18 paintbrushes in the classroom. 4 are lost during a lesson. How many paintbrushes are there now?

  b There are 9 yellow flowers and 7 red flowers in a pot. How many flowers are there in total?

# ⏻ 3c **Counting patterns**

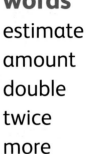

**Explore**

I think that there are about 12 chickens because I think that there are more than 10, but less than 15.

I think that there are about 8 chickens.

I think there are more than 15 chickens, but not as many as 20.

**Key words**
estimate
amount
double
twice
more
less

Without counting, what do you think?

# Subtracting numbers by counting back

## Learn

Look at these eggs, but do not count them.

Estimate how many eggs you think there are.

Count the eggs to work out the number.

It does not matter if your estimate is not the right amount. It just needs to be a close guess.

## Practise

1 Take a handful of beads but do not count them.
   Try to take these amounts.

   a Take about 6 beads.

   b Take about 10 beads.

   c Take about 15 beads.

2 Without counting, estimate each amount.
   Count to check if you were near your estimate.

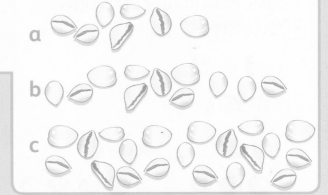

## Try this

Work with a partner.
Try to take about
15 cubes from a pile
without counting them.

Count your cubes.

Whose estimate was nearer to 15?

## Think like a mathematician

Put the beads on tens frames to help you count how many there are.

## Doubling numbers to 10

### Learn

The number of birds has doubled.
First there were 3. There are now twice as many.

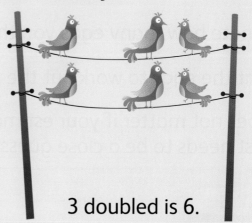

3 doubled is 6.

### Practise

1 Double the number of clay balls. How many balls have you made?

a

b

c

d

2 Double these numbers.

a ⟮ 1 ⟯   b ⟮ 5 ⟯

c ⟮ 6 ⟯   d ⟮ 8 ⟯

### Try this

If you hold up 2 fingers in a mirror you can see 4 fingers altogether.

How many do you see if you hold up 3 fingers?

How many do you see if you hold up 7 fingers?

What is the largest number you see using your fingers and the mirror?

# Counting on in ones and tens

## Learn

Count on in ones.

Count on in tens.

14 15 16 17 18

| 1 | 2 | 3 | 4 ● | 5 | 6 | 7 | 8 | 9 | 10 |
|---|---|---|---|---|---|---|---|---|---|
| 11 | 12 | 13 | 14 ● | 15 | 16 | 17 | 18 | 19 | 20 |
| 21 | 22 | 23 | 24 ● | 25 | 26 | 27 | 28 | 29 | 30 |
| 31 | 32 | 33 | 34 ● | 35 | 36 | 37 | 38 | 39 | 40 |
| 41 | 42 | 43 | 44 ● | 45 | 46 | 47 | 48 | 49 | 50 |

## Practise

1 Put five counters on a number square to show each sequence. What numbers do you cover up?

Count **back** in **ones** from **22**.
Count **on** in **tens** from **6**.

| 1 | 2 | 3 | 4 | 5 | ● | 7 | 8 | 9 | 10 |
|---|---|---|---|---|---|---|---|---|---|
| 11 | 12 | 13 | 14 | 15 | ● | 17 | ● | ● | ● |
| ● | ● | 23 | 24 | 25 | ● | 27 | 28 | 29 | 30 |
| 31 | 32 | 33 | 34 | 35 | ● | 37 | 38 | 39 | 40 |
| 41 | 42 | 43 | 44 | 45 | ● | 47 | 48 | 49 | 50 |

a Count on in ones from 12.
b Count on in ones from 34.
c Count back in ones from 20.
d Count on in tens from 10.
e Count back in tens from 60.
f Count on in tens from 23.

2 Copy and complete the patterns. Are you counting forwards or backwards? Are you counting in ones or in tens?

a 10  20 __ __ __ __ __
b 19  18 __ __ __ __ __
c 11 __ __ __  15 __ __
d 80 __  60 __ __ __ __

## Think like a mathematician

Use a hundred square to check that you are counting correctly. If you count in ones, you count along a row. If you count in tens you count up or down.

## Counting in twos

**Learn**

When we count in twos from zero, we say every other number.
2, 4, 6, 8, 10

Carry on counting in twos.

| ✗ | ② | ✗ | ④ | ✗ | ⑥ | ✗ | ⑧ | ✗ | ⑩ | 11 | 12 | 13 | 14 | **15** | **16** | 17 | 18 | **19** | 20 |

**Practise**

1 Use a pot of paint.
Take your fingers for
a walk. Which numbers
come next in the pattern?

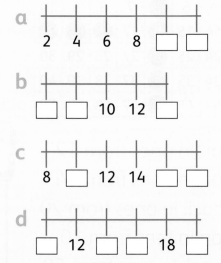

2 4 6 8 ☐ ☐

2 How many counters
will there be in the empty
frames?

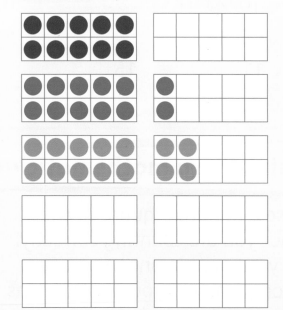

3 What are the missing numbers?

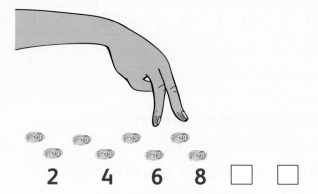

a
2 4 6 8 ☐ ☐

b
☐ ☐ 10 12 ☐

c
8 ☐ 12 14 ☐ ☐

d
☐ 12 ☐ ☐ 18 ☐

## Self-check

### A Numbers to 20

Count both groups and write down how many there are.
Which is the larger group?

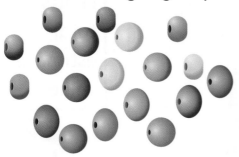
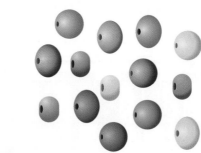

### B Addition and subtraction

**1** Which pairs make 10?

**2** How would you use this number line to work out 14 + 5?

**3** How would you use this number line to work out 18 − 3?

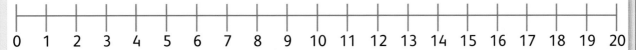

### C Counting patterns

**1** Take a handful of pencils. How many do you think you have?
Count to check.

**2** Use tens frames to help you double these numbers.

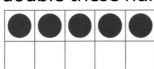

**a** Double 5 is __.
**b** Double 8 is __.
**c** Double 10 is __.

**3** Write the rule for each number pattern. What will the next number be?

**a**     　　**b**

## ⟳ 4a Money

**Explore**

Coins and notes are worth different amounts.
Do you know what each kind of coin is worth?

**Key words**
coin
cent(s)
total
estimate
value

I have eight 1 cent coins.

I have two 5 cent coins.

## Recognising and sorting coins

**Learn**

What is the same about these coins?
What is different?
Which would you rather have? Why?

1 cent

5 cents   is the same as

10 cents   is the same as

## Practise

Count the coins.

1 There are ___ 1 cent coins.

2 There are ___ 5 cent coins.

3 There are ___ 10 cent coins.

4 How many coins are there altogether?

## Making totals

### Learn

How much money is there altogether?

We can put them together and add.

4 cents and 2 cents make a total of 6 cents.

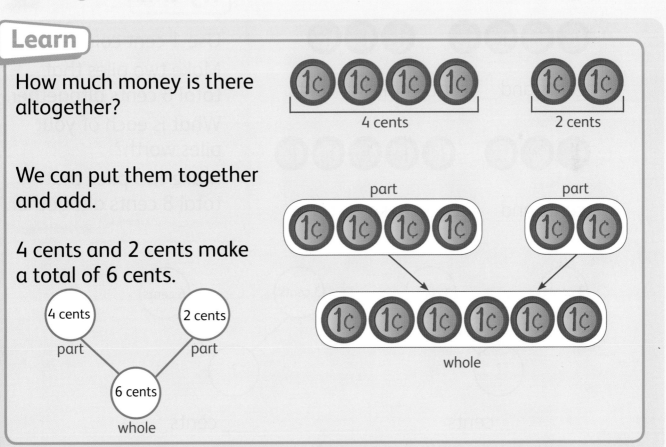

4 cents

2 cents

part

part

4 cents
part

2 cents
part

6 cents
whole

part

whole

## Practise

**1** Make these amounts using 1 cent coins. Write the totals.

a

b

c

d

**2** How much money is there altogether?

a

___ cents and ___ cents make ___ cents.

b

___ cents and ___ cents make ___ cents.

**Try this**

Use 1 cent coins.
Make two piles that total 6 cents altogether.
What is each of your piles worth?
Make two piles that total 8 cents altogether.

c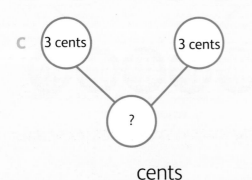

```
3 cents        3 cents
       \      /
        \    /
         ?
```

_____ cents

d
```
3 cents        6 cents
       \      /
        \    /
         ?
```

_____ cents

# How much do you estimate?

**Try this**

Georgia has 5 cents.

How many coins could she have?

## Learn

Estimate the total amount of money.

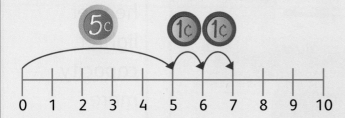

Sort the coins and then count them to check the total.

5 cents and 1 cent and 1 cent makes 7 cents.

## Practise

1 Take a handful of coins. Do not count them.

   a I estimate that I have taken ___ cents.

   b Use this number line to help you count the total of the coins you take.

0  1  2  3  4  5  6  7  8  9  10  11  12  13  14  15  16  17  18  19  20

   My coins total ___ cents.

2 Which of these estimates is better?

   a

   15 cents or 8 cents?

   b

   4 cents or 8 cents?

#  4b Measures

## Explore

measure
length
longer
shorter
weight
balance
heavier
lighter
capacity
more
less

What can we measure?

## Longer or shorter?

## Learn

Which looks longer?

We measure to find which is longer.

The blue pencil is longer than the red pencil. 10 cubes is more than 7 cubes.

## Practise

1

a Compare the length of these shapes. Which is shortest? Which is longest?

b Measure them with counters or cubes.

2 Which is longer?

a

b
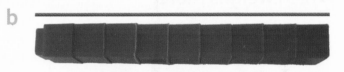

## Try this

Find objects around you that you think might be the same length.

Use hand spans to compare them.

## Think like a mathematician

Use the same kind of measurement when you measure two objects. If one string is 14 cubes and another string is 14 toy cars, you cannot compare them!

# Heavier or lighter?

Which is heavier?

Which feels heavier?

Which weighs more?

The apple is **heavier** than the banana because 9 cubes is **more** than 5 cubes.

1

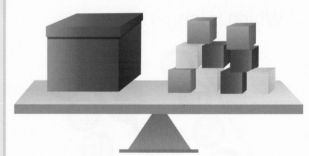

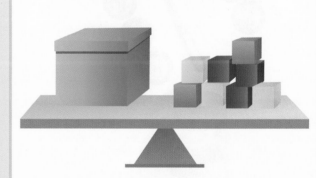

a Which box is heavier than the others?

b Which box is lighter than the others?

2 How many cubes does the green box weigh?

# Does it hold more or less?

**Learn**

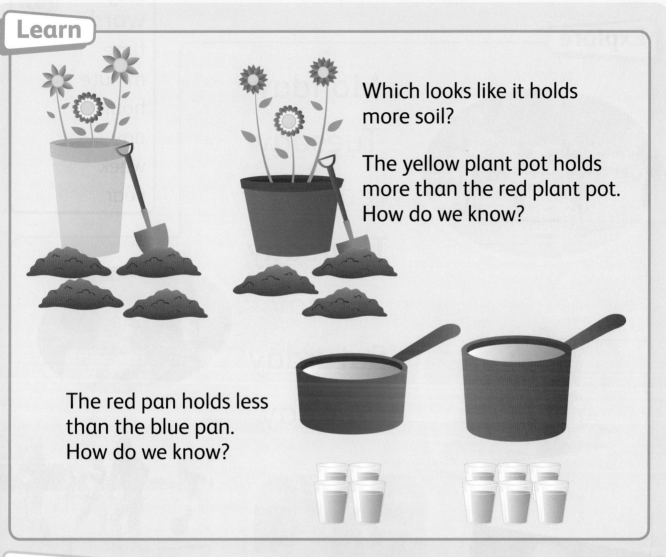

Which looks like it holds more soil?

The yellow plant pot holds more than the red plant pot. How do we know?

The red pan holds less than the blue pan. How do we know?

**Practise**

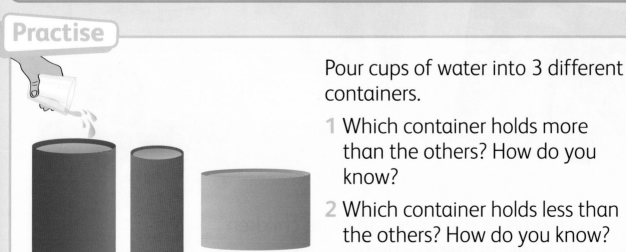

Pour cups of water into 3 different containers.

1 Which container holds more than the others? How do you know?

2 Which container holds less than the others? How do you know?

## 4c Time

**Explore**

Monday

Tuesday

Wednesday

**Thursday**

Friday

Saturday

Sunday

### Key words

time

minute

hour

day

week

year

On which days of the week could the children in the pictures do these activities?

# Measuring time

## Learn

We can measure time in different ways.

A tree takes a long time to grow.

We measure this in years.

An egg takes a short time to cook.

We measure this in minutes.

## Try this

Use a timer.
What can you do in one minute?

How many jumps can you do?

How many times can you bounce a ball?

How many numbers can you write?

## Practise

**1 a** What day is it today?　**b** What day was it yesterday?

　**c** What day is it tomorrow?　**d** How many days are there until Saturday?

**2** Copy and complete the sentences. Use the words below to help you fill in the missing time words.

( minutes )　( hours )　( days )　( week )　( months )　( years )

**a** This baby is 6 **m**_____ old.
　This boy is 6 **y**_____ old.

**b** The children have play time outside for 20 **m**_____.

**c** There are 24 **h**_____ in 1 day.
　There are 7 **d**_____ in
　1 **w**_____.

## Self-check

### A Money

Take a handful of coins.

1 Estimate how much money you have. Do not count it.

2 Sort the coins into piles of the same kind.

   a What kind of coin do you have the most of?

   b What kind of coin do you have the least of?

3 Use a number track to help you add the value of your coins. Was your estimate close?

### B Measures

Choose 3 different containers. Turn them on their sides.

1 Count how many cubes fit along the length of each container. Which one is the longest?

2 Count how many cubes each container weighs. Which container is the heaviest?

3 Count how many cups of water each container holds. Which container holds the most?

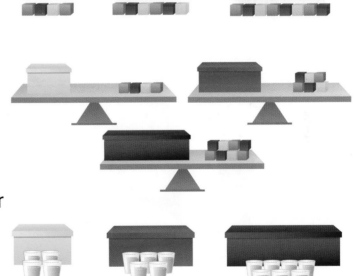

### C Time

1 Shuffle cards with the days of the week written on them.

2 Put the cards in order. Start with Monday.

3 How can you check if you are right?

## 5a Problem solving

### Problem 1

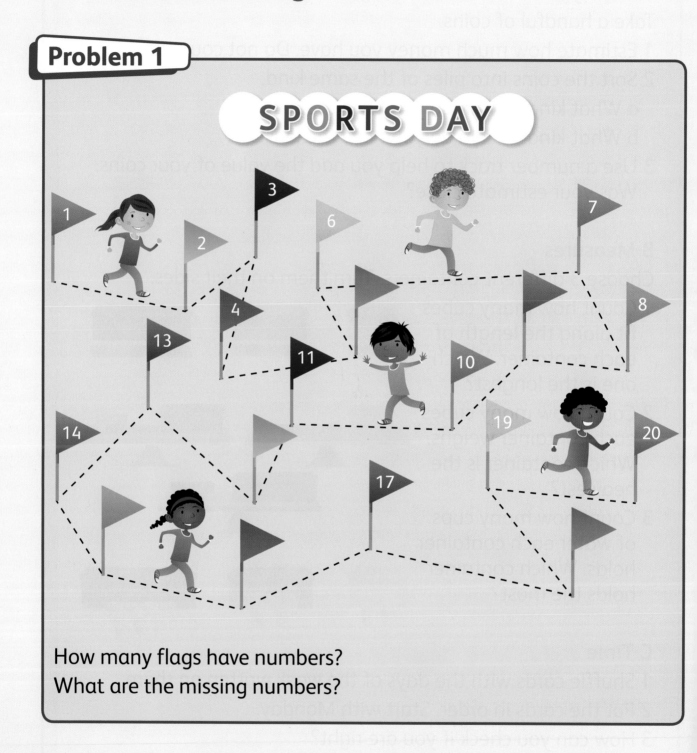

How many flags have numbers?
What are the missing numbers?

## Problem 2

Leandra and Osmay are throwing balls into a box.

Osmay has 16 throws and misses with 5 of the balls. How many balls does he get into the box?

## Problem 3

Leandra has 6 red balls and 6 yellow balls. She throws 3 of her red balls into the box. How many balls does she have left to throw?

## Problem 4

Who has made the longest jump?

How do you know?

## Problem 5

Draw pictures to help answer these.

12 children are balancing balls in a race. 4 of them drop their balls.
How many children are left in the race?

Alissa bounces a ball 16 times in a minute.
Asim bounces his ball three more times than Alissa.
How many times does Asim bounce his ball?

## Problem 6

A teacher is giving out stickers to the children to say, "Well done!"
They are different shapes and make a pattern on the sticker sheet.

Draw the next 3 shapes in the pattern.

## Problem 7

At the end of Sports Day, the results show that Class 1 scored 24 points.
Class 2 scored 17 points.

Choose objects to help you compare the two scores.
Show which score is more.

cubes     counting beads     a number track     counters

Which class won Sports Day?

# Unit 6  Number and problem solving

## 6a Counting patterns

### Explore

| 1 | 2 | 3 | 4 | 5 | 6 | 7 | 8 | 9 | 10 |
|---|---|---|---|---|---|---|---|---|---|
| 11 | 12 | 13 | 14 | 15 | 16 | 17 | 18 | 19 | 20 |
| 21 | 22 | 23 | 24 | 25 | 26 | 27 | 28 | 29 | 30 |
| 31 | 32 | 33 | 34 | 35 | 36 | 37 | 38 | 39 | 40 |
| 41 | 42 | 43 | 44 | 45 | 46 | 47 | 48 | 49 | 50 |
| 51 | 52 | 53 | 54 | 55 | 56 | 57 | 58 | 59 | 60 |
| 61 | 62 | 63 | 64 | 65 | 66 | 67 | 68 | 69 | 70 |
| 71 | 72 | 73 | 74 | 75 | 76 | 77 | 78 | 79 | 80 |
| 81 | 82 | 83 | 84 | 85 | 86 | 87 | 88 | 89 | 90 |
| 91 | 92 | 93 | 94 | 95 | 96 | 97 | 98 | 99 | 100 |

**Key words**

pattern
double
twice
more
less
odd
even

What do you notice about the painted numbers?

Which numbers will be painted next?

## Doubling numbers

### Learn

How many paint tins are there?

If we double the tins of paint, how many will there be?

There are now twice as many.
5 doubled is 10.

How many cubes are in the first chain?
How many cubes are in the second chain?

Double 7 is 14.

**Practise**

1  Make these cube chains. Then make a chain that is double the length.

a         b

c         d

2  Double these numbers. The first one has been done for you.

a  Double 1 is **2**.

b  Double 5 is ___.

c  Double 8 is ___.

d  Double 10 is ___.

3  Write the missing numbers?

a  3 doubled is ___.        b  4 doubled is ___.

c  7 doubled is ___.        d  10 doubled is ___.

# Counting in tens

## Learn

We can use tens rods to help count in tens.
Each rod is made up of ten cubes.

This rod shows 10.    Two tens rods make 20.    We add another rod each time we add another 10.

Here is a pattern that starts with 3.

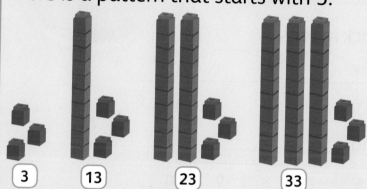

(3)    (13)    (23)    (33)

| 1 | 2 | 3 | 4 | 5 | 6 | 7 | 8 | 9 | 10 |
|---|---|---|---|---|---|---|---|---|---|
| 11 | 12 | 13 | 14 | 15 | 16 | 17 | 18 | 19 | 20 |
| 21 | 22 | 23 | 24 | 25 | 26 | 27 | 28 | 29 | 30 |
| 31 | 32 | 33 | 34 | 35 | 36 | 37 | 38 | 39 | 40 |

## Practise

1 Make each number using tens rods and ones cubes.

a Write the next two numbers.

b Write the next four numbers.

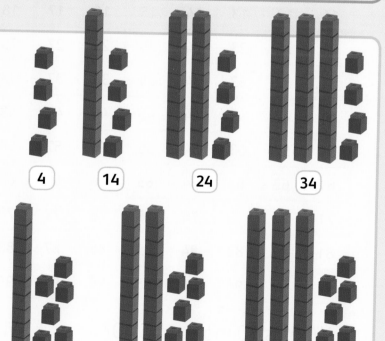

(4)    (14)    (24)    (34)

(6)    (16)    (26)    (36)

**2** Count in tens on the number lines.

**a** Start with 0 and count on in tens.

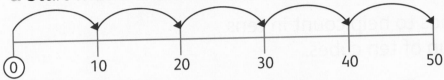

0    10    20    30    40    50

**b** Start with 1 and count on in tens.

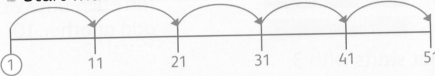

1    11    21    31    41    51

**c** Start with 50 and count back in tens.

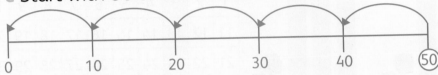

0    10    20    30    40    50

**3** Use counters on a number grid.

| 1 | 2 | 3 | 4 | 5 | 6 | 7 | 8 | 9 | 10 |
|---|---|---|---|---|---|---|---|---|---|
| 11 | 12 | 13 | 14 | 15 | 16 | 17 | 18 | 19 | 20 |
| 21 | 22 | 23 | 24 | 25 | 26 | 27 | 28 | 29 | 30 |
| 31 | 32 | 33 | 34 | 35 | 36 | 37 | 38 | 39 | 40 |
| 41 | 42 | 43 | 44 | 45 | 46 | 47 | 48 | 49 | 50 |
| 51 | 52 | 53 | 54 | 55 | 56 | 57 | 58 | 59 | 60 |
| 61 | 62 | 63 | 64 | 65 | 66 | 67 | 68 | 69 | 70 |
| 71 | 72 | 73 | 74 | 75 | 76 | 77 | 78 | 79 | 80 |
| 81 | 82 | 83 | 84 | 85 | 86 | 87 | 88 | 89 | 90 |
| 91 | 92 | 93 | 94 | 95 | 96 | 97 | 98 | 99 | 100 |

**a** What is 10 more than 40?     **b** What is 10 less than 30?

**c** Count in tens from 9 to 99.     **d** Count in tens from 3 to 93.

**4** Write the missing numbers.

a 1   11   21   ☐   ☐   51   ☐   71   81   ☐   101

b 6   16   ☐   ☐   ☐   56   ☐   76   ☐   ☐   ☐

c 2   12   22   ☐   ☐   ☐   ☐   ☐   ☐   ☐   ☐

d 105   95   85   ☐   ☐   55   ☐   35   ☐   ☐   5

e 103   93   83   73   ☐   ☐   ☐   33   23   ☐   3

## Counting in twos

**Learn**

Start with 2 and count in twos.

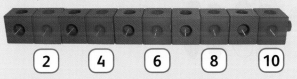

② ④ ⑥ ⑧ ⑩

Look at how the pattern continues to 20.

② ④ ⑥ ⑧ ⑩ ⑫ ⑭ ⑯ ⑱ ⑳

We call these numbers **even** numbers.
The numbers in between are called **odd** numbers.

Odd numbers

① ③ ⑤ ⑦ ⑨ ⑪ ⑬ ⑮ ⑰ ⑲

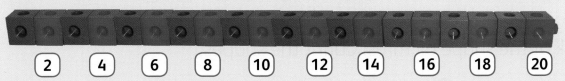

② ④ ⑥ ⑧ ⑩ ⑫ ⑭ ⑯ ⑱ ⑳

Even numbers

## Practise

1 Make these cube chains. Count in twos to practise each number pattern.

a

b

> Make a chain 20 cubes long.

2 Count in twos. How many are there?

a

b

c

3 Look at the shape pictures. Count the shapes.

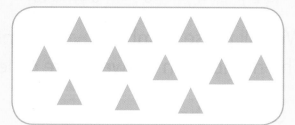

a There are ____ ●.
b There are ____ ▲.
c Which picture shows an even number?
d Which picture shows an odd number?

# ⟳ 6b Numbers

## Explore

Who has more?

**Key words**

more
less
partition
between
tens
ones

## Comparing numbers

### Learn

18  13  Which number is larger? Which number is smaller?

18 is **more** than 13. 13 is **less** than 18.

Name a number that is between 13 and 18.

| 1 | 2 | 3 | 4 | 5 | 6 | 7 | 8 | 9 | 10 | 11 | 12 | 13 | 14 | 15 | 16 | 17 | 18 | 19 | 20 |
|---|---|---|---|---|---|---|---|---|---|---|---|---|---|---|---|---|---|---|---|

15 is between 13 and 18. We can compare it to these numbers.

15 is **more** than 13, but **less** than 18.

### Practise

1 Use cubes to make a number between each pair of numbers.

  a  14  17        b  15  18        c  13  11

2 Use **more** or **less** to complete each sentence.

  a   is ____ than

   A number in between is ____.

  b   is ____ than

   A number in between is ____.

3 Copy and complete these statements.

  a    10

   10 more than 10 is __.

  b

   10 more than 20 is __.        10 less than 20 is __.

# Partitioning numbers

## Learn

This is a two-digit number.

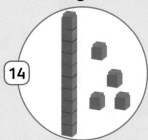

We can split two-digit numbers into tens and ones.

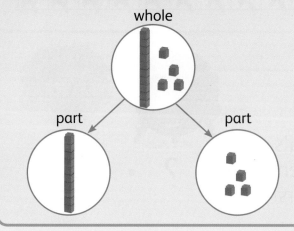

The whole number has been split into two parts.

We can use arrow cards to show this.

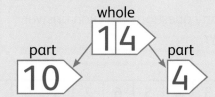

14 can be split into 10 and 4.

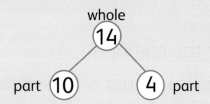

## Practise

1 Make each number with rods and cubes. Split it into two parts. What numbers can you make?

a 14    b 16    c 19

2 Make these numbers.

  a Which number will you make from the arrow cards 10▷ and 9▷?

  b Which two arrow cards will you use to make the number 1⎸7▷?

3 Copy and complete to show how numbers can be split.

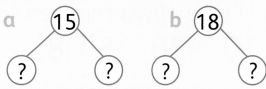

a (15)  ?  ?     b (18)  ?  ?

# Number problems and puzzles

## Learn

There are different ways to answer problems.

> Asim got 20 questions right in a test.
>
> Dion got 10 fewer questions right than Asim.
>
> How many questions did Dion answer correctly?

You can draw the number problem.

You can use a number track.

| 1 | 2 | 3 | 4 | 5 | 6 | 7 | 8 | 9 | 10 | 11 | 12 | 13 | 14 | 15 | 16 | 17 | 18 | 19 | 20 |
|---|---|---|---|---|---|---|---|---|----|----|----|----|----|----|----|----|----|----|----|

## Practise

1 Write the numbers.

   a Javel's number is 1 less than Anya's number. Anya's number is between 18 and 20. What are their numbers?

   b Javel's number is more than 22, but less than 28. What could his number be?

2 Write the different numbers you can make using these rods and cubes.

  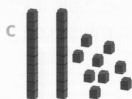

3 Write the different numbers you can make with these arrow cards.

10 > 20 > 5 > 8 >

4 Anja and Javel each tried to throw 20 balls into a bucket. Javel scored 12 and Anja got 5 fewer than Javel. How many balls did Anja get in the bucket?

## Self-check

### A Counting patterns

**1** Take a card from a pack of 1 to 5 number cards.

1  2  3  4  5

  **a** Make a tower of cubes double the size of the number on your card.

  **b** How tall is your tower?

**2** Make another tower double the size of your first tower.

  **a** How tall is your new tower?

  **b** Count in twos from your second number tower until you get to 20. What numbers did you say?

**3** Count on and back in tens.

  **a** Count in tens from 20 until you get to 100. What numbers did you say?

  **b** Count back in tens from 86 until you get to 6. What numbers did you say?

### B Numbers

**1** Take any two cards from a set of 1 to 20 number cards.

  **a** Which is more and which is less?

  **b** Find your numbers on a number track to check.

| 1 | 2 | 3 | 4 | 5 | 6 | 7 | 8 | 9 | 10 | 11 | 12 | 13 | 14 | 15 | 16 | 17 | 18 | 19 | 20 |

**2** For both of your number cards, write the number that is 1 less.

**3** Make your numbers using tens rods and ones cubes. How can you split (partition) your numbers into tens and ones?

# Unit 7 Handling data and problem solving

## 7a Sorting objects and shapes

**Explore**

**Key words**
sort
sides
face
hexagon
pentagon
prism

Jamie is sorting out his toys.
What rule does he have for each sorting hoop?

## Naming and sorting 2-D shapes

**Learn**

This is a pentagon.
It has 5 sides.

This is a triangle.
It has 3 sides.

This is a hexagon.
It has 6 sides.

We can sort 2-D shapes into different groups in a Venn diagram.

Shapes with curved sides cannot go into the group so they stay outside.

What do you think the rule is for this Venn diagram?

These shapes have been sorted in two different ways.

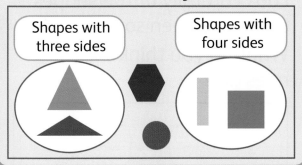

## Practise

1 Use a Venn diagram to sort 2-D shapes.

  a Sort shapes **with curved sides**.

  b Sort **triangles**.

  c Sort shapes **with four sides**.

  d Sort shapes that are **not squares**.

2 Look carefully at this Venn diagram. Where would you put these shapes?

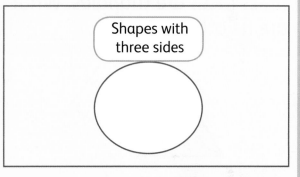

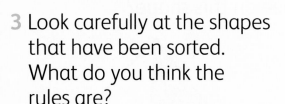

3 Look carefully at the shapes that have been sorted. What do you think the rules are?

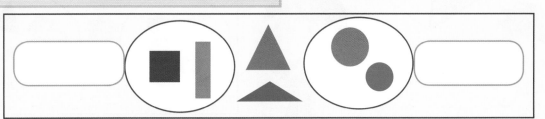

## Try this

Most 2-D shapes have corners. Some do not.

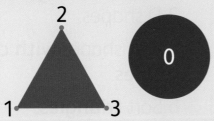

Find a way to sort your shapes by the number of corners they have.

## Naming and sorting 3-D shapes

## Learn

This is a triangular prism. Two of its faces are triangles. What are its other faces?

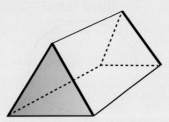

This is a triangular-based pyramid. What faces can you see on this shape?

We can sort 3-D shapes into different groups.

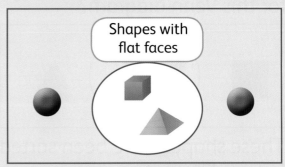

Shapes with flat faces

Look carefully at the shapes that have been sorted.

What do you think the rules are?

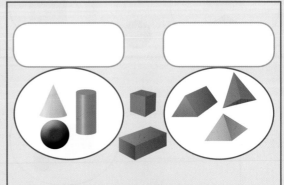

## Practise

1 Use a Venn diagram to sort 3-D shapes.

   a Sort shapes **with curved faces**.

   b Sort **pyramids**.

   c Sort shapes **with six faces**.

   d Sort shapes **that are not cylinders**.

2 Look carefully at this Venn diagram.

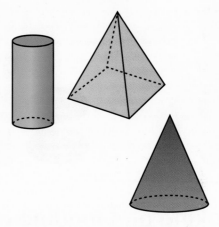

Shapes with square faces

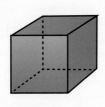

   Where would you put these shapes?

3 Look at the shapes in these Venn diagrams. What do you think the rules are?

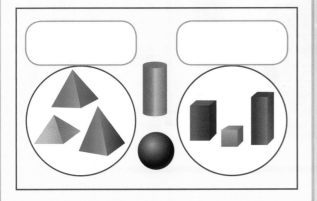

### Think like a mathematician

Turn a 3-D shape all around when you are looking at the different shapes of its faces or counting how many faces there are.

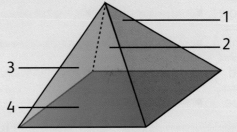

## Try this

What is the most common 3-D shape in your classroom?

## ⏱ 7b Pictograms

### Explore

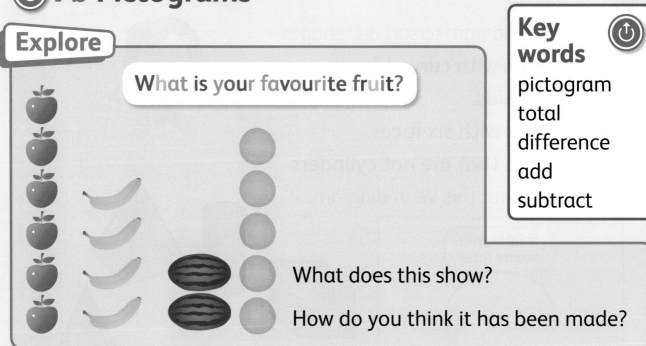

What is your favourite fruit?

What does this show?

How do you think it has been made?

## Making and reading pictograms

### Learn

A pictogram shows information using pictures or objects.

I want to find out the different colours of pencils I have.

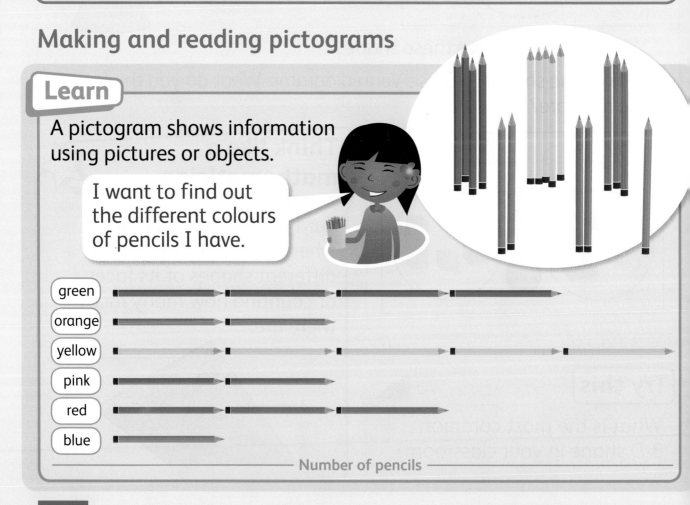

| | |
|---|---|
| green | |
| orange | |
| yellow | |
| pink | |
| red | |
| blue | |

Number of pencils

This pictogram shows the same information in a different way.

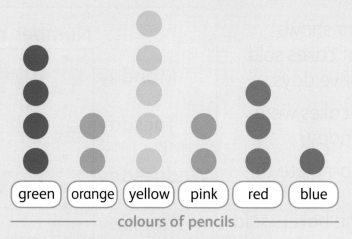

colours of pencils

How many of each colour are there?

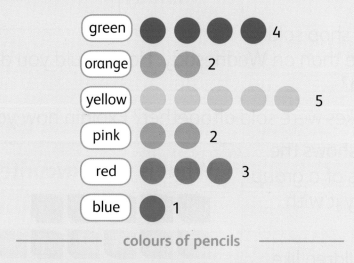

colours of pencils

How many pencils are there altogether?

What is the difference between the number of yellow pencils and green pencils?

Count up from the smaller number to the larger number.

## Practise

1 This pictogram shows the number of cakes sold by a baker in five days.

   a How many cakes were sold on Monday?

   b Copy and complete this sentence.
   On _____ the bakers sold two more cakes than on Tuesday.

   c On Friday, the shop sold one more cake than on Wednesday. How would you draw this on the pictogram?

   d How many cakes were sold altogether? Explain how you know.

**Number of cakes sold**

Monday

Tuesday

Wednesday

Thursday

Friday

2 This pictogram shows the favourite colours of a group of children. Copy it with coloured cubes.

   a How many children like each different colour?

   b There are two colours that three children like. What are they?

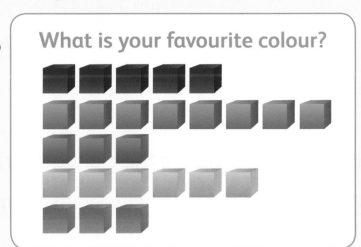

**What is your favourite colour?**

   c What is the difference between the number of children who like orange and the number of children who like yellow? How do you know?

   d How many more children like red than green?

   e How many children are in the group altogether? How did you work out the answer?

## Try this

Draw a pictogram to show the favourite drinks of the children in your class.

## Self-check

**A Sorting objects and shapes**

1 Look at these Venn diagrams.

2 Write two 2-D shapes that belong in the group and two shapes that do not.

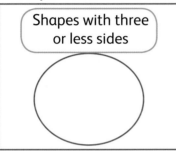

Shapes with three or less sides

3 Write down two 3-D shapes that belong in the group and two shapes that do not.

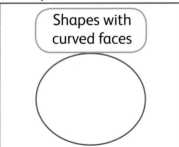

Shapes with curved faces

**B Pictograms**

1 Take two handfuls of coloured counters. Make a pictogram to show how many of each colour you have.

2 Write the number for each colour you have. What is the total number of counters? How do you know?

3 What is the difference between the most common and the least common colours? How do you know?

# Unit 8 Number and problem solving

## ⟳ 8a Addition

**Key words** ⟳
add
total
order

**Explore**

How can we work out how many t-shirts there are in the picture?

## Adding objects

**Learn**

We can put objects together to add them.

How many are in each part?

| 1 | 2 | 3 | 4 |

| 1 | 2 | 3 | 4 | 5 | 6 | 7 |

4 and 3 make 7.
4 + 3 = 7

80

## Practise

**1** Make each tower of cubes. Put them together to make one tall tower.
How many cubes are there altogether?

a   _____ + _____ = _____

b   _____ + _____ = _____

c   _____ + _____ = _____

d   _____ + _____ = _____

**2** Find each total.

a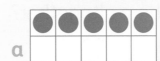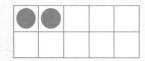

b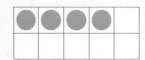

c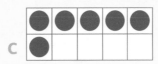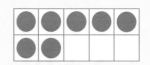

d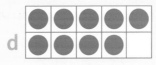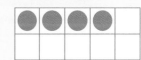

**3** Use cubes to model these additions.

a 4 + 3 = 7

b 6 + 3 = 9

c 8 + 4 = 12

d 9 + 6 = 15

## Checking your addition

How many are there altogether?

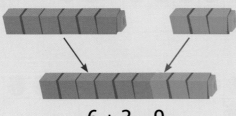

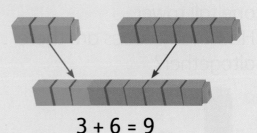

6 + 3 = 9          3 + 6 = 9

What do you notice?

# 3 + 6          =          6 + 3

 is the same as

**1** Use cubes to answer these.

a

2 + 3 = __ + __

b

__ + __ = 5 + 4

c

3 + __ = 7 + __

d

__ + 8 = __ + 5

**2** Answer these. The first one has been done for you.

a ● + ● ● ● ● ●    ● ● ● ● ● + ●

1 + 5 = 6    5 + 1 = 6

b ● ● ● ● + ● ● ● ● ● ●

___ + ___ = ___

● ● ● ● ● ● + ● ● ● ●

___ + ___ = ___

c ● ● ● ● ● ● ● + ● ● ● ● ● ●

___ + ___ = ___

● ● ● ● ● ● + ● ● ● ● ● ● ●

___ + ___ = ___

d ● ● ● ● ● ● ● ● + ● ● ● ● ● ● ● ● ●

___ + ___ = ___

● ● ● ● ● ● ● ● ● ● + ● ● ● ● ● ● ● ●

___ + ___ = ___

**3** Some of these additions are wrong! For each one, add the numbers in a different way to check.

a 4 + 6 = 10    b 7 + 5 = 13

c 5 + 9 = 15    d 8 + 7 = 15

e 5 + 12 = 19

Which questions are wrong?

**Try this**

What could the missing numbers be?

14 = __ + __

16 = __ + __

18 = __ + __

20 = __ + __

**8b Subtraction**

**Explore**

What is the same and what is different?

# Finding the difference

## Learn

How many more cubes are there in the taller tower?

2 more cubes are needed to make the towers the same height.

The difference between 5 and 3 is 2.

5 – 3 = 2

**Key words**
take away
subtract
difference

## Practise

1 Make each tower of cubes. What is the difference between the towers?

 a

 b

 c

 d

2 What is the difference between these numbers?

a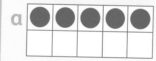

b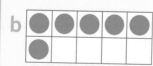

c

d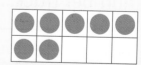

**3** Work out the difference for each day.

| Day | Daytime camels | Night-time camels |
|---|---|---|
| Monday | 6 | 3 |
| Tuesday | 8 | 5 |
| Wednesday | 9 | 4 |
| Thursday | 10 | 2 |

## Checking subtractions

### Learn

Here are 10 cubes.

If we take 3 away, how many are left?

There are 7 left.
10 − 3 = 7

Let us check!
We can start with 7 and add 3.
What do you notice?

We can also check on a number track.

| 1 | 2 | 3 | 4 | 5 | 6 | 7 | 8 | 9 | 10 |

### Practise

**1** Work out these subtractions with cubes.

Add on a number track to check your answers.

**a** 8 − 3 = ___

**b** 10 − 4 = ___

**c** 13 − 5 = ___

**d** 18 − 7 = ___

**e** 20 − 8 = ___

**f** 11 − 6 = ___

**2** Sabrina is adding to check some subtractions.

Write down each addition.

Which subtractions is she checking?

a
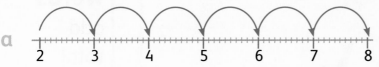

b
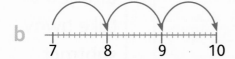

c
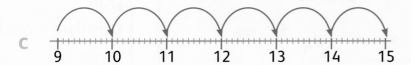

d
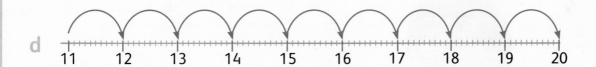

**3** Some of these subtractions are wrong! Use adding to check them.

a $9 - 5 = 4$     b $11 - 3 = 7$          c $14 - 5 = 9$

d $16 - 9 = 8$     e $18 - 9 = 8$

Which questions are wrong?

## Try this

Use adding to find Lev's mystery number.

$$\boxed{?} - 7 = 9$$

Make up your own mystery number question for a friend to answer.

# 8c Addition and subtraction

**Explore**

**Key words**
add
total
altogether
take away
subtract
pair
number bond
digit

What can you add and subtract?

# Using the +, – and = sign

## Learn

**Remember**

The = sign means is the same as.

The + sign is used when numbers are added together.

five      add      four      is the same as      nine

$$5 + 4 = 9$$

The – sign is used when numbers are taken away.

six      take away      two      is the same as      four

$$6 - 2 = 4$$

## Practise

1 Answer these.

a Emilio puts 4 seeds in one pot and 2 seeds in another pot. How many seeds does he plant altogether?

b 3 petals blew off this flower. How many petals are left?

2 Copy and write **+** or **−**.

a 5 ☐ 2 = 7

b 8 ☐ 5 = 3

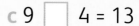

c 9 ☐ 4 = 13

d 10 ☐ 8 = 2

## Try this

Choose **+** or **−** then work out the answers.

Do you want to use **+** or **−** ?

6 ☐ 3 = __
9 ☐ 5 = __
6 ☐ 6 = __
10 ☐ 7 = __

## Think like a mathematician

Maths problems do not always have a **+** or **−** sign. Sometimes words tell you what to do. If a problem asks, "What is left?", you need to subtract the numbers.

# Number pairs

## Learn

Here are 10 counters.

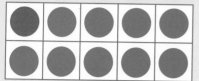

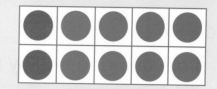

1 and 9 make 10.          What other ways do you know to make 10?

## Practise

1 Write an adding number fact for each of these flowers.
  The first one has been done for you.

a

1 + 7

b

___ + 6

c

3 + ___

d

___ + 4

e
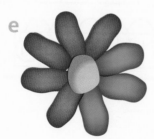
___ + 3

f

6 + ___

g

___ + 1

2 Change each addition fact into a subtraction.

a 8 + 1 = 9 ⟶ 9 − ☐ = __          b 7 + 2 = 9 ⟶ 9 − ☐ = __

c 6 + 3 = 9 ⟶ 9 − ☐ = __          d 5 + 4 = 9 ⟶ 9 − ☐ = __

# Different ways to add and subtract

## Learn

What is 6 add 13?

I am going to add by using a number track.

| 1 | 2 | 3 | 4 | 5 | 6 | 7 | 8 | 9 | 10 | 11 | 12 | 13 | 14 | 15 | 16 | 17 | 18 | 19 | 20 |

I am going to count on from the larger number.

| 1 | 2 | 3 | 4 | 5 | 6 | 7 | 8 | 9 | 10 | 11 | 12 | 13 | 14 | 15 | 16 | 17 | 18 | 19 | 20 |

I am going to model this using a tens frame.

What is 11 take away 5?

I am going to see how many jumps.

| 5 | 6 | 7 | 8 | 9 | 10 | 11 |

I am going to count back.

| 5 | 6 | 7 | 8 | 9 | 10 | 11 |

## Practise

1 Model these additions.

a 5 counters + 4 counters

b 4 counters + 8 counters

c 7 counters + 7 counters

d 6 counters + 9 counters

## Practise

2 Show how you can answer these.

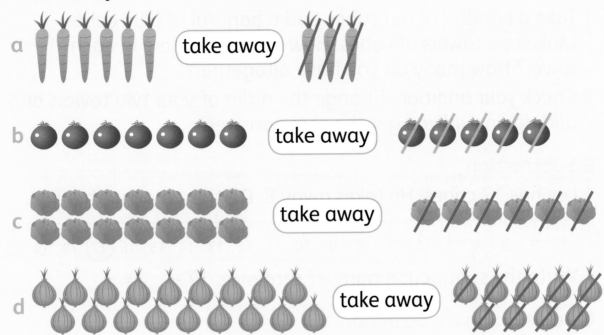

a    take away

b    take away

c    take away

d    take away

3 Add or subtract to solve these problems. The first one has been done for you.

    a Last month, Class 1 worked in the school garden for **8** days.
On **2** of the days it rained.
How many of the days had dry weather?
**8 − 2 = 6**
There were **6** days of dry weather.

    b It is Naomi's job to collect flower pots for planting seeds.
She finds **4** under a bench and **7** next to a tree.
How many flower pots does she find in total?

    c A group of **6** children help to water the flowers.
Another group of **6** children help to water the vegetables.
How many children help to water altogether?

    d Ajay has picked **7** cabbages from a row of **9**.
How many cabbages are left?

## Self-check

### A Addition

**1** Take a handful of red cubes and a handful of blue cubes. Make two towers of cubes. How many are there in each tower? How many do you have altogether?

**2** Check your addition. Change the order of your two towers and add again. Did you get the same answer?

### B Subtraction

**1** Lev has 17 cubes. He takes away 8. Do this on a number line.

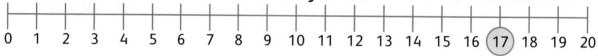

**2** Write the subtraction number sentence. $17 - \square = \underline{\quad}$

### C Addition and subtraction

**1** Write the addition and subtraction number sentences.

$12 + \square = 20$ $\qquad$ $\square - 8 = 12$

**2** Copy and complete using **+** or **−**.
a $11 \ \square \ 5 = 16$
b $15 \ \square \ 6 = 9$

**3** Solve this problem. Is it an addition or a subtraction? There are 7 children in the classroom. 2 children leave. How many children are left?

# Unit 9 Measure and problem solving

## ⟳ 9a Money

Explore

What coins could the girl have?

Who has enough money to buy a pineapple?

## Using coins to make totals

Learn

Each coin has a different value.

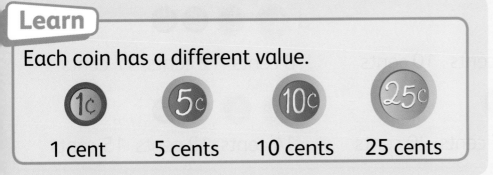

| 1 cent | 5 cents | 10 cents | 25 cents |

### Key words ⟳

coin
cents
exchange
value
estimate
total

95

Different coins can be put together to make different totals.

We can make 6 cents using a 5 cent coin and a 1 cent coin.

Count on from the largest value coin.

part — 1¢     part — 5¢

6 cents

6c

whole

0  1  2  3  4  5  6  7  8  9  10  11  12  13  14  15  16  17  18  19  20

## Think like a mathematician

If you have to add two coins, choose the coin with the larger value and count on from it.

## Try this

Lev has four coins. He says "I have 16 cents altogether."

Maya says "It is impossible to make 16 cents using four coins."

Is she right? Why do you think this?

## Practise

1 Which of these amounts can you make from the coins?

a   5¢ 1¢ 1¢ 1¢

   4 cents   7 cents   6 cents

b   10¢ 1¢ 1¢

   8 cents   11 cents   10 cents

d

   8 cents   12 cents   17 cents

c   10¢ 5¢ 5¢

   15 cents   17 cents   20 cents

e

   14 cents   12 cents   15 cents

**2** How can you make these amounts?

a

b

c

d

6 cents

11 cents

15 cents

20 cents

## Making totals in different ways

**Learn**

Coins can be used to make totals in different ways.
Count to find the totals.

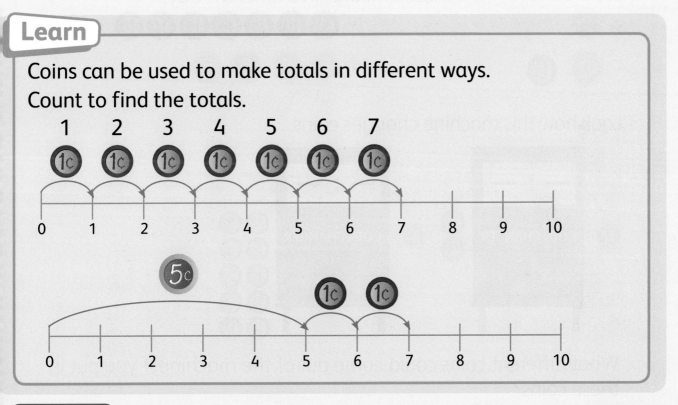

**Try this**

Maya has 15 cents.
She can make this amount using these coins.

She can also use these coins.
How many different ways can you make 15 cents using coins?

**Practise**

1 Write the amount for each money bag.

a

b

c

d

☐ cents ☐ cents ☐ cents ☐ cents

2 Draw coins to make these amounts in a different way.

a   b

c    d

3 Look how this machine changes coins.

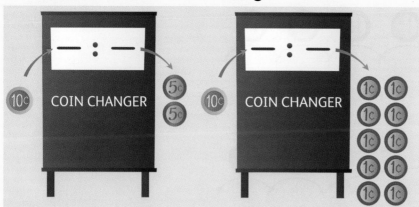

What different coins could come out of the machine if you put in these coins?

a eight 1 cent coins

b a 10 cent coin and three 1 cent coins

c three 5 cent coins and a 1 cent coin

# 9b Measures

## Explore

Which is longer, the pink and blue fish or the crab? How do you know?

Which bag of fish food is heavier?
How do you know?

How could you find out which fish tank holds more water?

**Key words**

measure
length
weight
capacity
longer
shorter
longest
shortest
more
less
estimate
unit

## Comparing length

**Learn**

Which looks longer?

You can measure to find out which is longer.

**Try this**

Lev has no cubes to measure these pieces of string.

How could he use buttons instead?

How is this the same and how is it different from using cubes?

## Practise

1 How many cubes fit along the length of each fish?

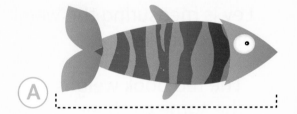

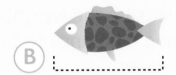

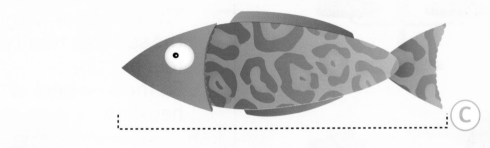

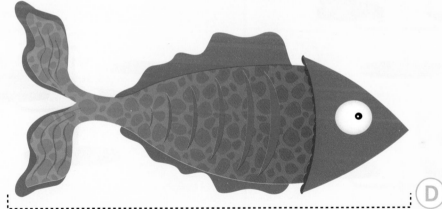

2 Which fish is the shortest?

3 Which fish is the longest?

4 Copy and complete these sentences.
  Use the words longer than or shorter than.

a Fish B is _____ _____ Fish C.    b Fish A is _____ _____ Fish B.
c Fish D is _____ _____ Fish A.    d Fish C is _____ _____ Fish D.

## Comparing weight

### Learn

You can measure the weight of objects using a balance to find which is heavier.

Count the weights to see how heavy each object is.

### Try this

Lev is measuring the weight of two books.

The red book weighs the same as three wooden blocks.
The blue book weighs the same as twenty-four pencils.
So the blue book is heaviest.

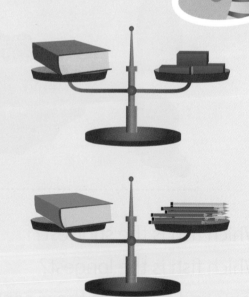

What mistake has Lev made?

How would you help him to compare the weights?

## Practise

1 Copy and complete the sentences.

   a __ is the lightest bag.

   b __ is the heaviest bag.

2 Copy and complete these sentences.
   Use the words **heavier than** or **lighter than.**

   a Bag A is _____ _____ Bag C.    b Bag D is _____ _____ Bag A.
   c Bag B is _____ _____ Bag D.    d Bag C is _____ _____ Bag B.

# Comparing capacity

Which container looks like it holds the most?

You can measure the capacity of containers using jugs of water.

Container C holds the most jugs of water.

**1** How many jugs of water does each tank hold?

a Tank __ holds the least.

b Tank __ holds the most.

2 Complete these sentences. Use the words holds more than or holds less than.

a Tank A ___ ___ ___ Tank D.

b Tank C ___ ___ ___ Tank B.

3 Put the tanks in order.

___ ___ ___ ___

Most                    Least

## Try this

Maya is comparing the capacity of two plastic boxes.

The blue box holds three jugs of water. The yellow box holds twelve glasses of water. So the yellow box holds more.

What mistakes has Maya made?

How can you help her to measure the capacity correctly?

105

# 9c Time

**Explore**

Which of these happens first in the week?

Which of these happens earliest in the day?

**Key words**

day
week
month
Monday
Tuesday
Wednesday
Thursday
Friday
Saturday
Sunday
before
after
o'clock
minute hand
hour hand

# Days and months

## Learn

It is important to know the order of the days of the week.

There are seven days in a week. Try to remember all seven names!

Friday comes after Thursday.

Monday comes before Tuesday.

Wednesday is around the middle of the week.

There are twelve months in a year.

- January
- February
- March
- **April**
- May
- June
- July
- **August**
- September
- October
- November
- **December**

## Practise

1 Use a calendar to write these days of the week.
   a Tuesday comes after _____.
   b Friday comes after _____.
   c Wednesday comes before _____.
   d Monday comes before _____.

## Think like a mathematician

The days of the week keep going round and round. When Sunday ends, it is back to Monday again!

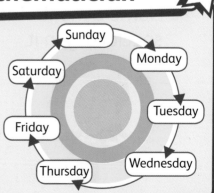

Sunday
Monday
Tuesday
Wednesday
Thursday
Friday
Saturday

## Practise

**2**

| January | February | March |
|---|---|---|
| April | May | June |
| July | August | September |
| October | November | December |

**a** Name the first month of the year.

**b** Name the month that comes before July.

**c** Name the last month of the year.

**d** Name the month between March and May.

**e** Name a month that has a special day in it.

**3** Here are the different things that happen to Samir during one week.

Put them in the right order.

Sunday

Tuesday

Wednesday

Saturday

Thursday

Friday

Monday

# O'clock times

## Learn

We can tell the time using a clock.

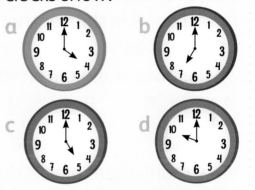

There are two hands on a clock.

The big hand points to the number of minutes.

The small hand points to the number of hours.

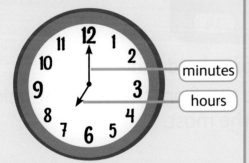

minutes

hours

When the minute hand points to the 12 we say the time is o' clock.

This clock shows that the time is three o'clock.

## Practise

1 Use a clock to make these o'clock times.

   a one o'clock    b three o'clock

   c nine o'clock    d eleven o'clock

2 What o'clock times do these clocks show?

## Try this

Poppy says that there are two different o'clock times where the hands on the clock make a straight line.

What are they?

## Self-check

### A Money

1 Take a handful of coins. Sort them in groups of the same kind of coins. What is each kind of coin worth?

2 Make 6 cents with coins. Do this in two different ways.

3 How many different ways can you make 10 cents?

### B Measures

1 Maya is measuring two leaves using cubes. Leaf A is 15 cubes long. Leaf B is shorter than Leaf A. Does leaf B measure more or less cubes?

2 These boxes hold different amounts of blocks.

A   B   C

How many more blocks does Box A hold than Box C?

3 Put the three boxes in order. Do this from the box that holds the least to the one that holds the most.

### C Time

1 Take 12 counters.

Put a counter on a table for each month of the year that you can say.

How many months did you remember? Use a calendar to say the names of the months you still need to learn.

2 What time does this clock show?

3 Copy this clock. Draw the big hand and small hand to show that it is 9 o'clock.

# Unit 10 Problem solving and review

## 10a Problem solving

### Problem 1

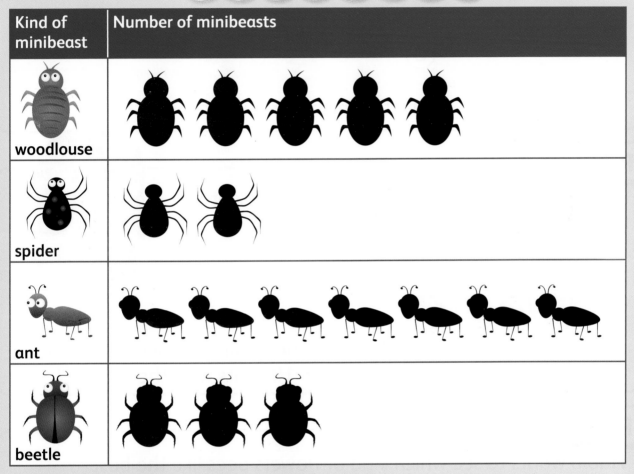

**MINIBEASTS**

| Kind of minibeast | Number of minibeasts |
|---|---|
| woodlouse | |
| spider | |
| ant | |
| beetle | |

Class 1 are doing a project on minibeasts.

They look under rocks to find different minibeasts.

Aziza draws this pictogram to show what was under her rock.

**1** Which minibeast was there most of?

**2** How many more woodlice were there than beetles?

**3** How many minibeasts were under Aziza's rock in total?

## Problem 2

Sadiki finds three worms under his rock.

Measure these worms.

Which worm is the shortest? Which worm is the longest?

## Problem 3

Lulu wants to buy a magnifying glass to look at
the minibeasts.
They cost 10 cents each.
These are the coins that Lulu has:

How many different ways can Lulu
make 10 cents with these coins?

## Problem 4

Habib wants to see which kind of flowers bees like the best.

He has three different flowers.

He puts the flowers in this order:

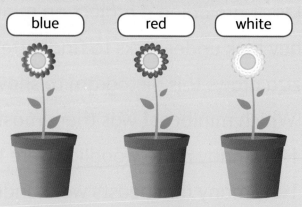

What other ways can Habib
put them in order?

## Problem 5

Class 1 keep a record of the number of caterpillars they find during a week.

On Monday they find 4 caterpillars.
On Tuesday they find 9 caterpillars.

How many caterpillars is that altogether?

On Wednesday they find 3 caterpillars.
On Thursday they find 10 caterpillars.

What is the difference between these numbers of caterpillars?

## Problem 6

There are 16 butterflies in a field. 7 fly off.
How many butterflies are left?

Is the answer an odd number or an even number of butterflies?

## Problem 7

Spiders have eight legs.
Flies have six legs.

Zahara is drawing a picture of a fly in a spider's web.
How many legs will she need to draw altogether?

## Problem 8

This ladybird has the same amount of dots on each wing.

Double the dots on the wings of these ladybirds so that each wing has the same amount.

Ⓐ     Ⓑ     Ⓒ

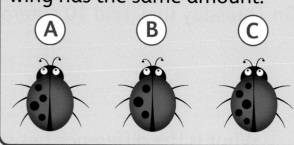

## Problem 9

These three children have each made a "minibeast hotel" out of twigs, leaves and stones.

I counted 10 minibeasts in my bug hotel.

I counted 18 minibeasts.

I counted 10 more than Isoke.

Isoke

Ebo

Barika

How many minibeasts visited Barika's bug hotel?

# Unit 11 Number and problem solving

## ⏻ 11a Counting patterns

### Explore

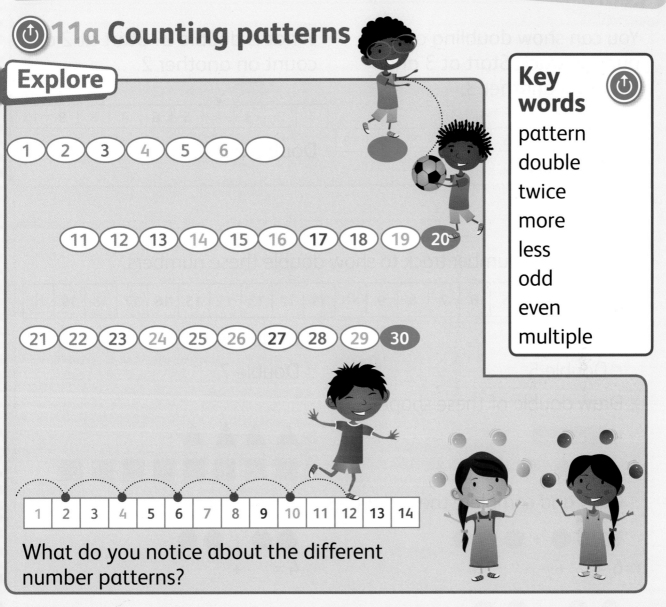

**Key words** ⏻

Key words
pattern
double
twice
more
less
odd
even
multiple

1  2  3  4  5  6

11  12  13  14  15  16  17  18  19  20

21  22  23  24  25  26  27  28  29  30

| 1 | 2 | 3 | 4 | 5 | 6 | 7 | 8 | 9 | 10 | 11 | 12 | 13 | 14 |

What do you notice about the different number patterns?

## Doubling numbers

### Learn

Doubling a number is the same as adding the same number twice.

I have three juggling balls.

I have another three balls. We have six altogether.

## Learn

You can show doubling on a number track. Start at 3 and count on another 3.

| 1 | 2 | 3 | 4 | 5 | 6 | 7 | 8 | 9 | 10 |

Double 3 is 6.

What is double 2? Start at 2 and count on another 2.

| 1 | 2 | 3 | 4 | 5 | 6 | 7 | 8 | 9 | 10 |

Double 2 is 4.

## Practise

1 Hop on the number track to show double these numbers.

| 1 | 2 | 3 | 4 | 5 | 6 | 7 | 8 | 9 | 10 | 11 | 12 | 13 | 14 | 15 | 16 | 17 | 18 | 19 | 20 |

   a Double 2               b Double 3

   c Double 5               d Double 7

2 Draw double of these shapes.

   a        b

   c 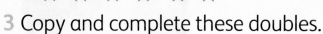       d

3 Copy and complete these doubles.

a 6 = __ + __          b 4 = __ + __

c 10 = __ + __

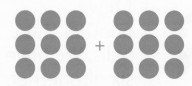

d 18 = __ + __

## Think like a mathematician

Double  is

Double  is

# Counting in twos

## Learn

Counting in twos is as easy as saying every other number.

**2**    **3**    **4**    **5**    **6**

Say    Think    Say    Think    Say

(Even) numbers ⟶ 2    4    6    8    10    12    14    16    18    20

(Odd) numbers ⟶    3    5    7    9    11    13    15    17    19

## Practise

1 Count on from each number in twos. What number do you end on?
The first one has been done for you.

a 2    4    6    8    [10]

b [14]    ☐

c [1]    ☐

d [6]    ☐

2 Which three numbers come next?

a
| 2 | 4 | 6 | 8 | | | |

b
| 20 | 18 | 16 | 14 | | | |

c
| 8 | 10 | 12 | 14 | | | |

d
| 1 | 3 | 5 | 7 | | | |

## Think like a mathematician

If you count in twos from an odd
number, the pattern will always be odd.
If you count in twos from an even
number, the pattern will always be even.

## Counting in tens

When we count in tens we make a pattern. What do you notice?

We can use a hundred grid to help spot tens patterns.

| 1 | 2 | 3 | 4 | 5 | 6 | 7 | 8 | 9 | 10 |
|---|---|---|---|---|---|---|---|---|---|
| 11 | 12 | 13 | 14 | 15 | 16 | 17 | 18 | 19 | 20 |
| 21 | 22 | 23 | 24 | 25 | 26 | 27 | 28 | 29 | 30 |
| 31 | 32 | 33 | 34 | 35 | 36 | 37 | 38 | 39 | 40 |
| 41 | 42 | 43 | 44 | 45 | 46 | 47 | 48 | 49 | 50 |
| 51 | 52 | 53 | 54 | 55 | 56 | 57 | 58 | 59 | 60 |
| 61 | 62 | 63 | 64 | 65 | 66 | 67 | 68 | 69 | 70 |
| 71 | 72 | 73 | 74 | 75 | 76 | 77 | 78 | 79 | 80 |
| 81 | 82 | 83 | 84 | 85 | 86 | 87 | 88 | 89 | 90 |
| 91 | 92 | 93 | 94 | 95 | 96 | 97 | 98 | 99 | 100 |

**Practise**

1 Make each number using tens rods and ones cubes.
   Then count in tens for three more numbers.

   a 10     b 13     c 16     d 25

2 Count on and back in tens on the number square.

   a Start with 16 and count on in tens.

   b Start with 100 and count back in tens.

3 Which three numbers come next?

   a
| 10 | 20 | 30 | 40 | | | |
|---|---|---|---|---|---|---|

   b
| 100 | 90 | 80 | 70 | | | |
|---|---|---|---|---|---|---|

   c
| 16 | 26 | 36 | 46 | | | |
|---|---|---|---|---|---|---|

   d
| 3 | 13 | 23 | 33 | | | |
|---|---|---|---|---|---|---|

# Multiples of 2 and 10

## Learn

Every **even** number is a **multiple of 2**. Multiples of 2 always end in **2, 4, 6, 8** or **0**.

Multiples of **10** always end in a **0**.

| 1 | 2 | 3 | 4 | 5 | 6 | 7 | 8 | 9 | 10 |
|----|----|----|----|----|----|----|----|----|-----|
| 11 | 12 | 13 | 14 | 15 | 16 | 17 | 18 | 19 | 20 |
| 21 | 22 | 23 | 24 | 25 | 26 | 27 | 28 | 29 | 30 |
| 31 | 32 | 33 | 34 | 35 | 36 | 37 | 38 | 39 | 40 |
| 41 | 42 | 43 | 44 | 45 | 46 | 47 | 48 | 49 | 50 |
| 51 | 52 | 53 | 54 | 55 | 56 | 57 | 58 | 59 | 60 |
| 61 | 62 | 63 | 64 | 65 | 66 | 67 | 68 | 69 | 70 |
| 71 | 72 | 73 | 74 | 75 | 76 | 77 | 78 | 79 | 80 |
| 81 | 82 | 83 | 84 | 85 | 86 | 87 | 88 | 89 | 90 |
| 91 | 92 | 93 | 94 | 95 | 96 | 97 | 98 | 99 | 100 |

## Practise

1 Are these numbers of cubes multiples of 2?

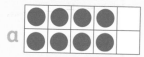

a 10 cubes    b 20 cubes    c 17 cubes

2 Now make towers of 10 cubes. Are they multiples of 10?

3 Write the numbers. Say if they are multiples of 2 or 10.

a

__ is a multiple of __.

b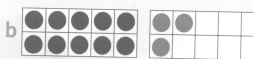

__ is not a multiple of __.

c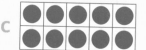

__ is a multiple of 2 and 10.

4 (20) (15) (12) (8) (1) (10) (6) (14) (30) (18) (17) (9)

a Which numbers are multiples of 2?

b Which numbers are not multiples of 2 or 10?

# 11b **Numbers**

**Explore**

Which number came first in the race?
Which number comes first on a number line?

**Key words**

more
less
bigger
smaller
same
different
order
first
second
third
partition
tens
ones

## Comparing numbers

**Learn**

My number is more than your number.

My number is less than yours.

Which is more, 12 or 8?

## Learn

Find a number that is between 8 and 12.
11 is between 8 and 12. It is more than 8, but less than 12.

My number is between 8 and 12.

Look at these pairs of numbers.

What is the same about them? What is different?

## Practise

1 Use the number track to find a number between each pair
of numbers.

| 1 | 2 | 3 | 4 | 5 | 6 | 7 | 8 | 9 | 10 |
|---|---|---|---|---|---|---|---|---|---|
| 11 | 12 | 13 | 14 | 15 | 16 | 17 | 18 | 19 | 20 |

a 4 and 9          b 8 and 13
c 11 and 18        d 14 and 17

2 Compare each number using **more than** or **less than**.
The first one has been done for you.

a

**8** is **more than** 5.

b

_____ is more than _____.

c

_____ is more than _____.

d

_____ is more than _____.

3 Look at these number pairs. What is the same? What is different?

a ③ and ⑧    ⑤ and ⑩    b ② and ⑩    ⑳ and ⑫

c ⑥ and ⑱    ⑭ and ⑯    d ⑲ and ⑮    ⑬ and ⑰

**Think like a mathematician**

14 has more on
So 14 is bigger
than 12.

We can use tens rods and cubes to help compare numbers.

14 has **1 ten** and **4 ones**          12 has **1 ten** and **2 ones**

# Ordering numbers

## Learn

15  4  18  12

The smallest number is 4. All the other numbers are larger.

4      15  18  12

The next smallest number is 12 because 15 and 18 are larger than 12.

4  12      15  18

The correct order from smallest to largest is 4, 12, 15, 18.

## Practise

**1** Make each number out of cubes.
Put them in order from smallest to largest.

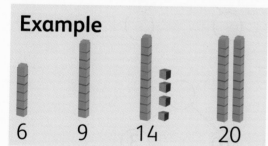

**Example**

6    9    14    20

a 15, 7, 14, 10

b 17, 13, 12, 16

c 18, 9, 11, 20

d 19, 8, 10, 6

**2** These numbers are in order from smallest to largest.

6  9  12  16  17

a Which is the first number?  b Which is the last number?

c In which position is the number 9?

**3** Put these groups of numbers in order from smallest to largest.

a 14, 10, 2, 18        b 19, 12, 10, 16        c 13, 9, 11, 12

# Partitioning numbers

16 = 10 + 6

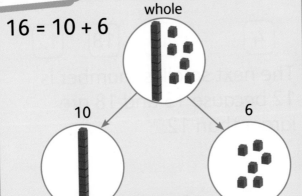

We can split whole numbers into two parts.

**Practise**

**1** Use cubes to spilt these numbers into two parts.

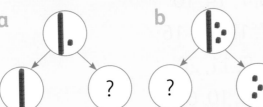

**2** Use only these arrow cards:

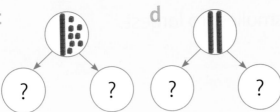

Write the numbers you can make that are less than 20.

**3** Partition these numbers. The first one has been done for you.

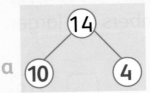

a

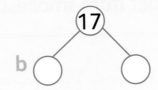

b

17

c

11

d

10    3

e

10    9

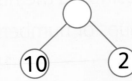

f    10    2

124

# Think like a mathematician

You can partition any number greater than 1.
3 can be partitioned into 2 and 1.
25 can be partitioned into 2 tens and 5 ones or 20 and 5.

## Try this

Khaled makes a number using a tens rod and an odd amount of ones cubes.

Is his number odd or even?

What numbers could it be?

## Self-check

**A Counting patterns**

Use number cards from 1 to 10.

1 Take an odd number.

2 Take the number 10 and count in tens to 100.

3 Take a multiple of 2 and count in twos to 20.

**B Numbers**

Take two cards from a set of 1 to 20 cards. Put them in order using counters on a number track.

1 Which number comes second?

2 Write a number that comes in between.

3 Choose a number. Show how it can be partitioned.
   Make it out of rods and cubes.

# Unit 12 Handling data and problem solving

## 12a Sorting numbers

**Explore**

**Key words**

sort
odd
even
Venn diagram
Carroll diagram
bigger
smaller

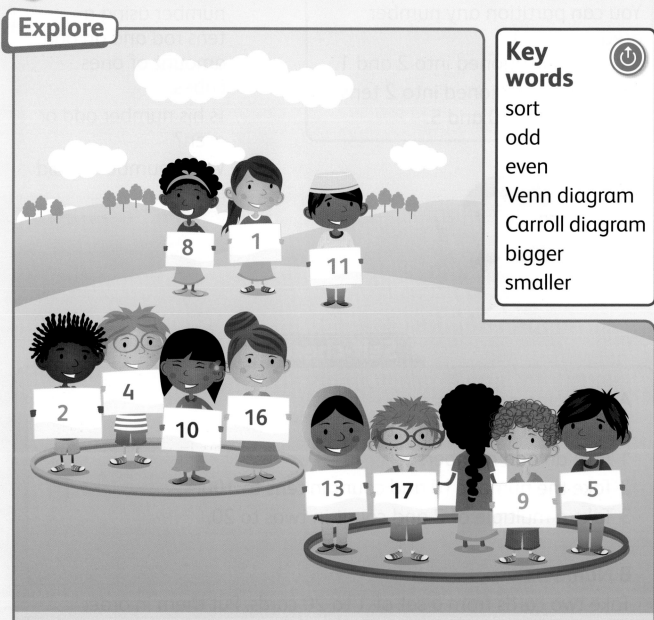

Can you help the three children outside the circles?
Help them to know where their numbers belong.

What are the rules for sorting the numbers into each circle?
Why do you think this?

# Odd or even?

## Learn

Make lines of two cubes. How many are left over?

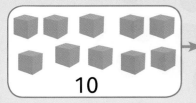

10

There are none left. 10 is even!

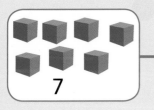

7

There is one left. 7 is odd!

Use a Venn diagram to sort numbers.

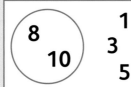

The numbers in the circle are even numbers.

Look how these numbers have been sorted: 1, 12, 3, 4, 2, 16

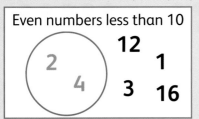

Even numbers less than 10

2
4
12
1
3
16

## Practise

1 Are these numbers odd or even? The first one has been done for you.

a

**5** is an **odd** number.

b

___ is an _____ number.

c

___ is an _____ number.

2 Make a stripey snake out of 20 cubes.

a What colour are the odd numbers in your snake?

b Point to the 15th cube. Is it odd or even?

3 Copy the Venn diagram. Sort the numbers.

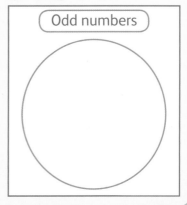

16
19
3
13
9
20

Odd numbers

127

## Bigger or smaller?

**Learn**

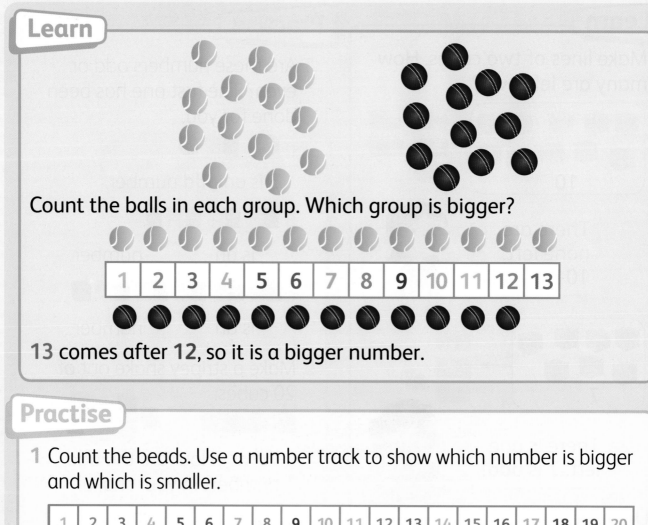

Count the balls in each group. Which group is bigger?

| 1 | 2 | 3 | 4 | 5 | 6 | 7 | 8 | 9 | 10 | 11 | 12 | 13 |

**13** comes after **12**, so it is a bigger number.

**Practise**

1 Count the beads. Use a number track to show which number is bigger and which is smaller.

| 1 | 2 | 3 | 4 | 5 | 6 | 7 | 8 | 9 | 10 | 11 | 12 | 13 | 14 | 15 | 16 | 17 | 18 | 19 | 20 |

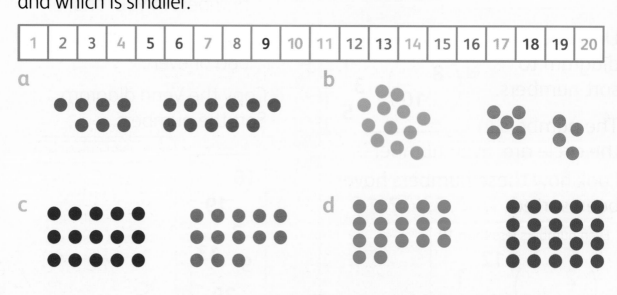

**2** Count each group.
Explain how you know which number is bigger and which is smaller.
The first one has been done for you.

a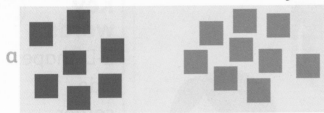

There are **2 less** green squares than orange squares.

b

There are ___ ____ blue circles than yellow circles.

c

There is ___ ____ pink star than white stars.

## Sorting numbers

Look how these numbers have been sorted on this Carroll diagram.

| More than 10 | Less than 10 |
|---|---|
| 13  14  18  15 | 7  5  2 |

The same numbers are now sorted differently.

| Odd numbers | Even numbers |
|---|---|
| 13  5  7  15 | 14  18  2 |

Copy this Carroll diagram.
Write the numbers in the correct block.

15  8
10  16
7  9
20

| Less than 11 | More than 11 |
|---|---|
|  |  |

# ⏻ 12b Sorting shapes

**Explore**

**Key words**

2-D shapes
side
corner
3-D shapes
face

## Sorting 2-D shapes

**Learn**

We can sort 2-D shapes by looking at their sides and corners.

This square has four sides. Each side is the same length.

This rectangle has four sides. Not all the sides are the same length.

Circles have one curved side.
Circles do not have corners.

2-D shapes with straight sides
have corners. A corner is where
two straight sides meet at a
point. Triangles have three
corners.

## Learn

We can use a Venn diagram
to sort shapes by their
number of sides.

Shapes with three sides

## Practise

Copy this Venn diagram. Sort the shapes.
The first one is done for you.

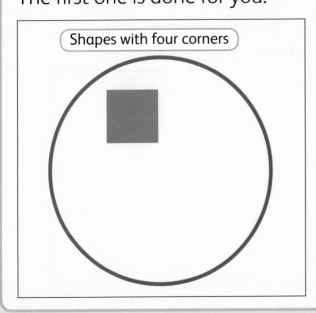

Shapes with four corners

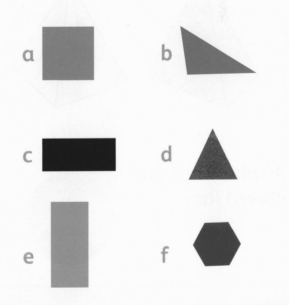

a

b

c

d

e

f

# Sorting 3-D shapes

## Learn

Cubes have six faces. They are all the same size and are squares.

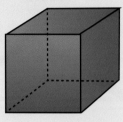

These shapes have curved and flat faces.

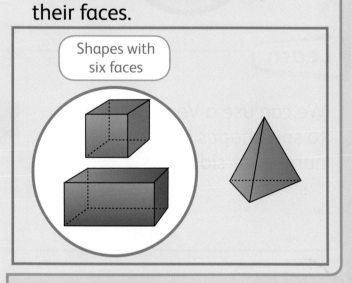

We can use a Venn diagram to sort shapes by their faces.

Shapes with six faces

Cuboids also have six faces. Not all the faces are the same shape.

These are pyramids.

This has 4 faces.     This has 5 faces.

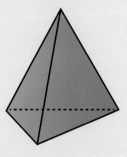

A sphere has one curved face.

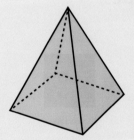

## Practise

Collect some 3-D shapes. Sort your shapes on a Venn diagram like this.

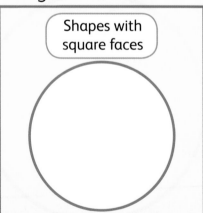

Shapes with square faces

# ⟳ 12c Block graphs

**Explore**

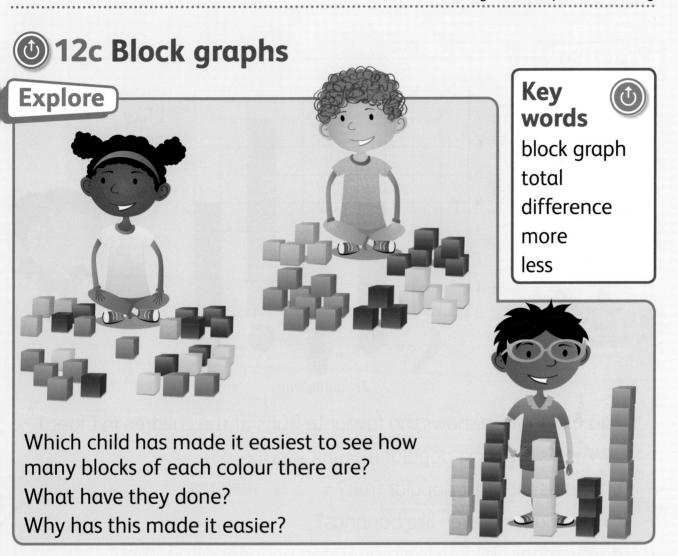

**Key words**

block graph
total
difference
more
less

Which child has made it easiest to see how many blocks of each colour there are?

What have they done?

Why has this made it easier?

## Making block graphs

**Learn**

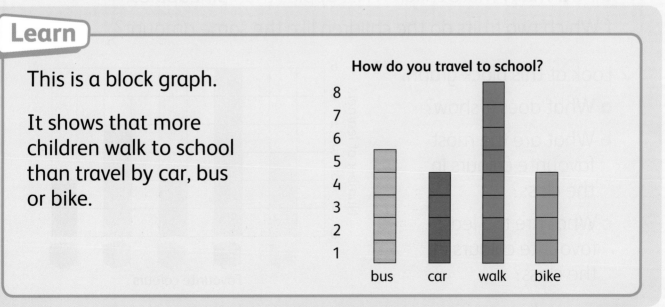

This is a block graph.

It shows that more children walk to school than travel by car, bus or bike.

**How do you travel to school?**

| 8 | | | | |
| 7 | | | | |
| 6 | | | | |
| 5 | | | | |
| 4 | | | | |
| 3 | | | | |
| 2 | | | | |
| 1 | | | | |
| | bus | car | walk | bike |

Practise

I like apples the most.

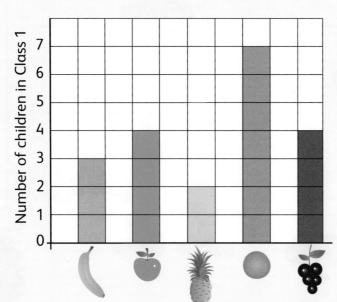

Number of children in Class 1

Favourite fruits

I like oranges the most.

**1** This block graph shows the favourite fruits of the children in Class 1.

   **a** What is the most popular fruit in Class 1?

   **b** What is the least popular fruit?

   **c** How many children like bananas?

   **d** How many children like grapes and bananas altogether?

   **e** How many more children like apples than pineapples?

   **f** Which two fruits do the children like the same amount?

**2** Look at this block graph.

   **a** What does it show?

   **b** What are the most favourite colours in the class?

   **c** What are the least favourite colours in the class?

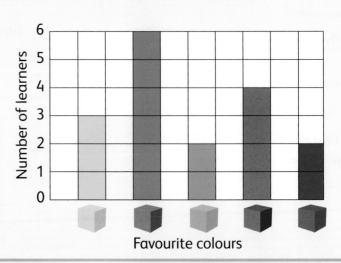

Number of learners

Favourite colours

## Self-check

### A Sorting numbers

1 Which is bigger? 16 17

2 Which is smaller? 12 18

3 Write these numbers correctly on the Carroll diagram.

9  15  6  10  19  3  11  20

| More than 14 | Less than 14 |
|---|---|
|  |  |

### B Sorting shapes

1 Take five 2-D shapes. Copy this Venn diagram and draw the shapes.

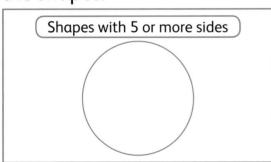

Shapes with 5 or more sides

2 Take five 3-D shapes. Copy this Carroll diagram and draw the shapes.

| Has a square face | No square faces |
|---|---|
|  |  |

### C Block graphs

1 Count the number of learners for each colour. Use cubes to make a block graph to show them.

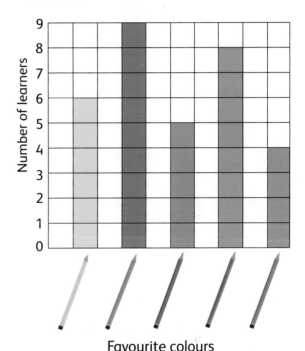

Favourite colours

2 What are the most and least common colours?

3 What is the difference between the number of yellow pencils and green pencils?

## 13a Addition and subtraction

**Explore**

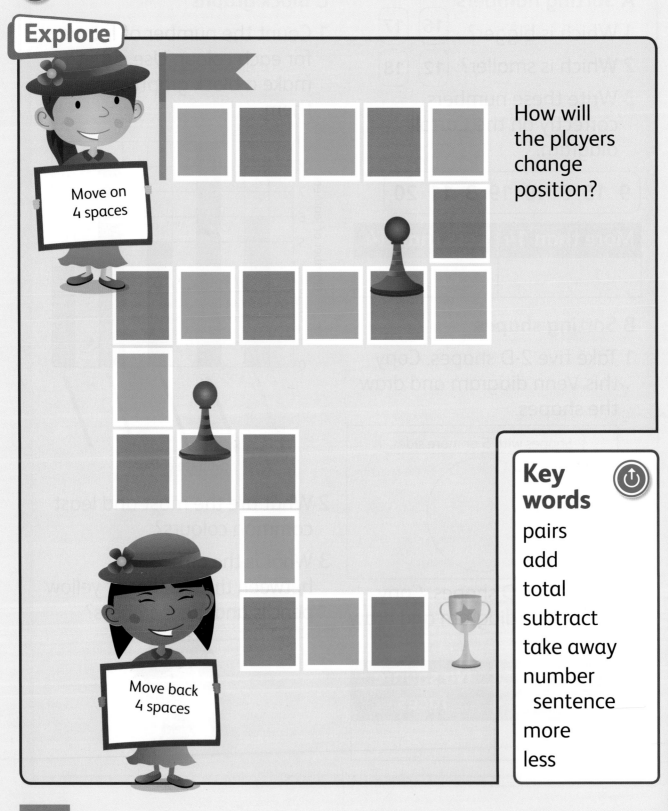

Move on
4 spaces

Move back
4 spaces

How will
the players
change
position?

**Key words**
pairs
add
total
subtract
take away
number
 sentence
more
less

# Using 10 to help

## Learn

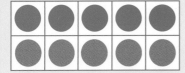 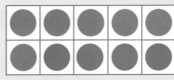 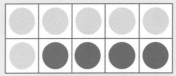

5 and 5 make 10       6 + 4 = 10       10 − 6 = 4

We can use pairs that make 10 to help work out our answer by looking for them in the question.

8    +    2    +    6 = ☐

Find a pair that make 10.
**8** and **2** make 10.

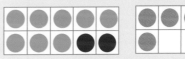

10 and **6** make 16, so
**8** + **2** + **6** = 16.

## Practise

1 Write an addition and subtraction for each pair of hands. The first one has been done for you.

a
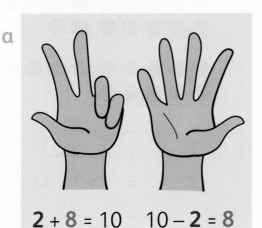

**2** + **8** = 10    10 − **2** = **8**

b
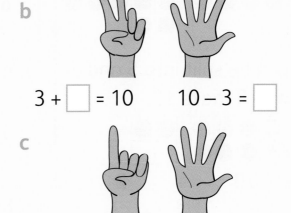

3 + ☐ = 10      10 − 3 = ☐

c

☐ + ☐ = 10      10 − ☐ = ☐

**2** Use cubes to add these numbers.

1 + 4 + 9

1 + 4 + 9 = 14

a

b

c

d

e

---

## Learn

We can also use pairs that make 10 to help by **splitting up numbers**.

5 + 7 = ☐

Split one of these numbers to help make 10.

5 + 7

7 can be split into 5 and 2. 5 and 5 make 10.

10 + 2

10 and 2 make 12, so 5 + 7 = 12.

---

## Practise

The answers to these questions are more than 10. Split up the second number to make 10 with the first number.

**1** 6 + 5 = ☐

**2** 7 + 6 = ☐

**3** 9 + 8 = ☐

**4** 8 + 6 = ☐

**5** 7 + 5 = ☐
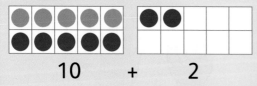
7  8  9  10  11  12

**6** 8 + 4 = ☐
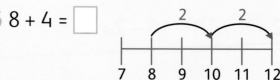
7  8  9  10  11  12

# Missing number questions

## Learn

16 + ☐ = 19

16 add something makes 19.

Count on from 16 until you get to 19.

| 1 | 2 | 3 | 4 | 5 | 6 | 7 | 8 | 9 | 10 | 11 | 12 | 13 | 14 | 15 | 16 | 17 | 18 | 19 | 20 |

| 19 |
| 16 | ? |

16 + 3 = 19

## Practise

1 Work out the missing numbers.

a

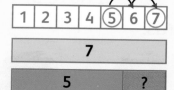

5 + ☐ = 7

b

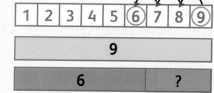

9 − ☐ = 6

c

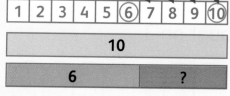

6 + ☐ = 10

d

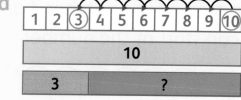

10 − ☐ = 3

| 1 | 2 | 3 | 4 | 5 | 6 | 7 | 8 | ⑨ | 10 | 11 | 12 | 13 | 14 | 15 | ⑯ |

**16**

**9** | **?**

$$9 + \boxed{\phantom{0}} = 16$$

**2** Lev has written some number sentences on the board. Maya has rubbed some off!

What are the missing numbers?

Explain how you found them.

$7 + \text{—} = 16$

$\text{—} + 7 = 12$

$\text{—} - 7 = 12$

$7 - \text{—} = 3$

## Counting on

**Learn**

To add numbers together, we can count forwards.

I have 16 apples. How many apples do we have altogether?

I have 3 apples.

We can start at the number 3 and count on 16.
Or we can start at the number 16 and count on 3.

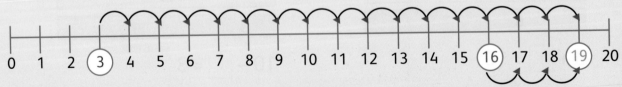

You can add the numbers in any order. You will always get the same answer. But it is faster to count on from the larger number.

## Practise

Use cubes to add the numbers in two different ways.

1 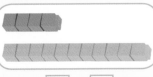 is the same as

$11 + 4$     =     □ + □

2  is the same as

$5 + 12$     =     □ + □

3 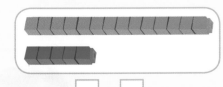 is the same as

$6 +$ □     =     $12 +$ □

4 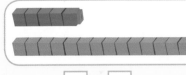 is the same as

□ + □     =     □ + □

## Taking away on a numberline

### Learn

Say the first number. Then jump backwards as you take away the second number.

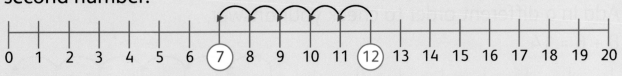

$12 - 5 = 7$

Start with the bigger number when you take away.

## Practise

**1** Count back on the number line to work out the answers.

   **a** 11 − 4 = ☐        **b** 12 − 4 = ☐

   **c** 13 − 4 = ☐        **d** 14 − 4 = ☐

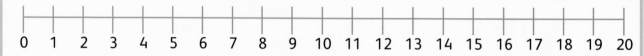

**2** Count on and back on the number line to work out the answers.

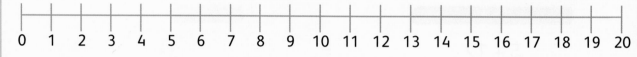

   **a** 13 − 5 = ☐       **b** ☐ + 5 = 13

   **c** 16 + ☐ = 19      **d** ☐ − ☐ = 16

## Checking your calculations

### Learn

I want to check an addition.

Just add the numbers in a different order. If they make the same answer, you are right!

6 + 8 = 14

Add in a different order to check your answer.

8 + 6 = 14

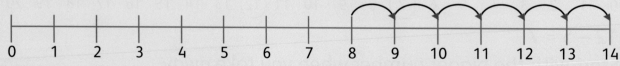

## Learn

Start with the bigger number when you subtract two numbers.

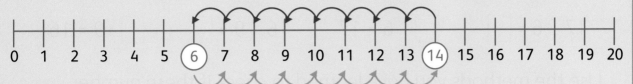

14 − 8 = 6

Add the numbers to check your answer.

6 + 8 = 14

## Practise

1 Count on a number line to add the numbers in two different ways.

a

4  5  6  7  8  9  10

5 + 4 = ☐        4 + 5 = ☐

b

6  7  8  9  10  11  12

7 + 5 = ☐        5 + 7 = ☐

c

12  13  14  15  16  17  18

12 + 6 = ☐      6 + 12 = ☐

d

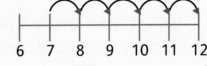

9  10  11  12  13  14  15  15

9 + 7 = ☐        7 + 9 = ☐

2 Use a number line to work out these subtractions. Add to check your answers.

a

4  5  6  7  8  9  10

7 − 2 = ☐        ☐ + 2 = 7

b

5  6  7  8  9  10  11

11 − 6 = ☐       6 + 5 = ☐

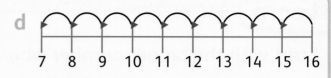

c

11 12 13 14 15 16 17

17 − 6 = ☐          ☐ + 6 = 17

d

7 8 9 10 11 12 13 14 15 16

16 − 9 = ☐          ☐ + 9 = 16

3 Use the methods you have learned to check if these number sentences are right or wrong.

a 7 + 9 = 15          b 5 + 14 = 19          c 15 − 8 = 6

Which number sentences are wrong?

**Try this**

You can check a take away question by moving the numbers and doing a different take away.

11 − 4 = ☐

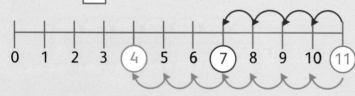

0 1 2 3 (4) 5 6 (7) 8 9 10 (11)

11 − 7 = ☐

Try other take away questions like this on a number line.

**Think like a mathematician**

Adding and taking away are opposites.

You can check 14 + 5 = 19 by working backwards and doing the opposite 19 − 5 = 14.

# 13b Doubles and halves

## Explore

Look at the numbers of things to eat.
What is happening to them?

## More doubling numbers

## Learn

Double 4 is the same as asking, "What is 4 + 4?"

The number of biscuits has doubled. There are twice as many. 4 doubled is 8.

## Practise

1 Double each of these.

a           b

c

d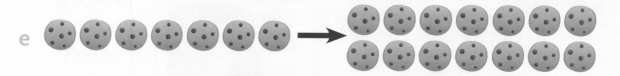

e

2 Complete these doubles. Use a number track to help.

| 1 | 2 | 3 | 4 | 5 | 6 | 7 | 8 | 9 | 10 | 11 | 12 | 13 | 14 | 15 | 16 | 17 | 18 | 19 | 20 |

a 2 + 2 = __          b 8 doubled is __.

c 10 + 10 = __          d Double 9 is __.

## Finding doubles and near doubles

## Learn

Double 4 makes 8.          4 + 5 = 9

Double 5 makes 10.          4 + 4 is a double.

          4 + 5 is a near double because
it is one more than 4 + 4.

## Practise

**1** Use counters to work out the answer.

a
4 + 4          4 + 5 = ☐

b
6 + 6          6 + 7 = ☐

c
7 + 7          7 + 8 = ☐

d
8 + 8          8 + 9 = ☐

**2** Work out each doubling fact. Then add 1 to work out the answer.

a 3 + 3 = ☐
3 + 4 = ☐

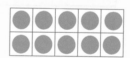

b 5 + 5 = ☐
5 + 6 = ☐

c 10 + 10 = ☐
10 + 11 = ☐

**3** Which double facts can help work out these near doubles?

a 2 + 3          b 5 + 6          c 7 + 6          d 9 + 8          e 9 + 10

# Finding half of a group of objects

## Learn

Here are 12 shells shared into two groups.

These groups are equal, so you have found half.
Half of 12 is 6.

Here are 15 shells shared into two groups.

These groups are not equal.
You cannot share 15 equally into two groups.

## Practise

1 Halve the dots on these folded papers.

a

Half of 6 = ☐

b
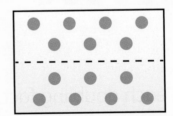

Half of 14 = ☐

c
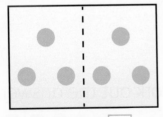

Half of 10 = ☐

d
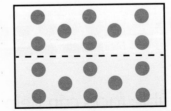

Half of 16 = ☐

**2** What halving fact does each picture show?
The first one has been done for you.
Use counters to check that your fact is correct.

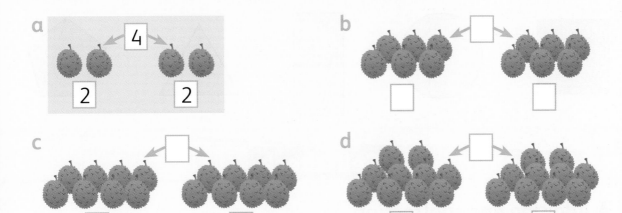

a

4

2          2

b

c

d

**3** Share objects into two groups to work out if the numbers
are odd or even.

a 9      b 16      c 17      d 20

# Finding half of shapes

**Learn**

You can fold the shape once in half like this:

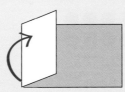

Each part is the same size.
It shows a half.

This shape has not been
folded in half.

## Practise

These shapes have been folded once.
Which shapes show half? Which do not? Why?

  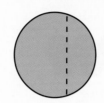  

## Self-check

### A Addition and subtraction

**1** Use the tens frame to work out 6 + 5.
First make 10 and then add 1 more.

**2** Maya says that 19 take away 7 is 13. Use the number line to check if she is right.

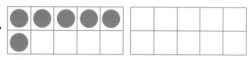

0  1  2  3  4  5  6  7  8  9  10  11  12  13  14  15  16  17  18  19  20

**3**   What is the missing number?

18

12    ?

$12 + \boxed{\phantom{0}} = 18$

### B Doubles and halves

**1** Take a handful of cubes. Share them into two groups. Do you think you took an odd or an even number of cubes? How do you know?

**2** Share 18 cubes into two equal groups. What is half of 18?

**3**

6 + 6        $6 + 7 = \boxed{\phantom{0}}$

## ⟳ 14a Money

**Explore**

20c notepads

17c highlighters

STATIONERY

10c pencils

6c erasers

What questions could you ask about these children and the items for sale?

**Key words** ⟳

cents
exchange
value
estimate
total
more
less

## Solving money problems

**Learn**

Hira has a 1 cent coin and two 5 cent coins.
She can add the coins together to find the total.

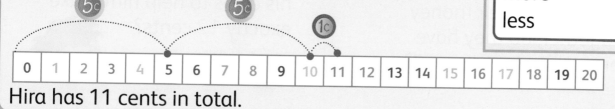

Hira has 11 cents in total.

## Practise

1 Use coins to model each problem.

  a On a table there is a 5 cent coin and four 1 cent coins.
  How much money is there altogether?

  b Jayraj wants to buy a bag of raisins for 10 cents. He does not
  have a 10 cent coin.
  Which coins can he use instead?

  c Rohini has 12 cents in her pocket. Make this amount in two
  different ways.

2 Irini has 10 cents altogether. She has more than one coin.
Draw the coins that Irini might have.

In what other ways can you make 10 cents?

| | |
|---|---|
| 10c | 5c  5c |
| 10c | |
| 10c | |

---

**Try this**

Lev has 12 cents. Maya has
7 cents. The cost of a pencil
is 20 cents.

If they put their money
together, do they have
enough to buy a pencil?

**Try this**

Samir wants to give his
brother exactly 12 cents.
How can he exchange one of
his coins to help him make
exactly 12 cents?

# ⏻ 14b Measures

**Explore**

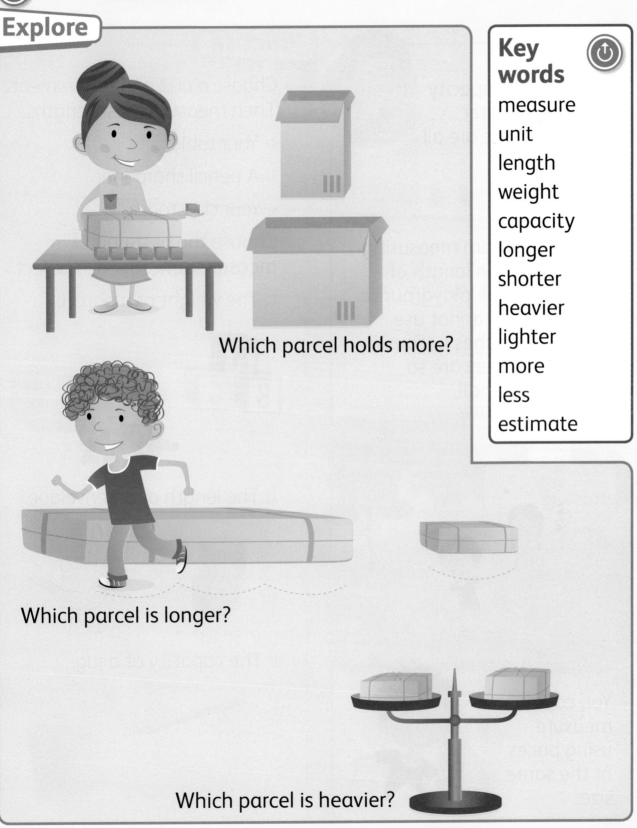

Which parcel holds more?

Which parcel is longer?

Which parcel is heavier?

**Key words** ⏻
measure
unit
length
weight
capacity
longer
shorter
heavier
lighter
more
less
estimate

# Choosing units to measure with

## Learn

I can measure capacity using cups of water because the cups are all the same size.

I am measuring the length of the playground. I cannot use cubes because they are so small.

You could measure using paces of the same size.

## Practise

1 Choose a unit of measurement. Then measure these lengths.

   a Your table

   b A pencil sharpener

   c Your classroom

2 Choose the best unit of measurement for each object.

   a The weight of a parcel.

   b The length of an envelope.

   c The capacity of a jug.

**3** Kofi is comparing the length of these parcels.

What is wrong? Why?

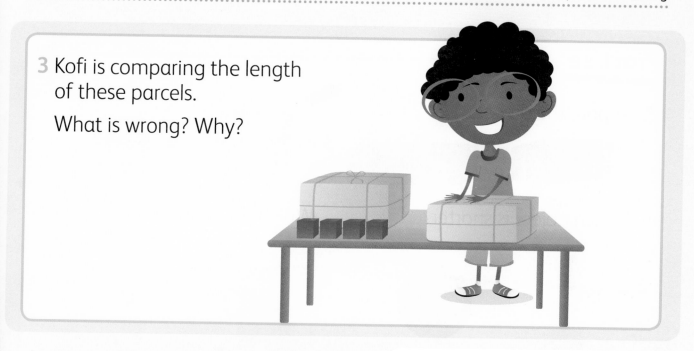

## Comparing measurements

> My parcel is 20 cubes long. We cannot compare their lengths because cubes and hand spans are different units.

**Learn**

> My parcel is 3 hand spans long.

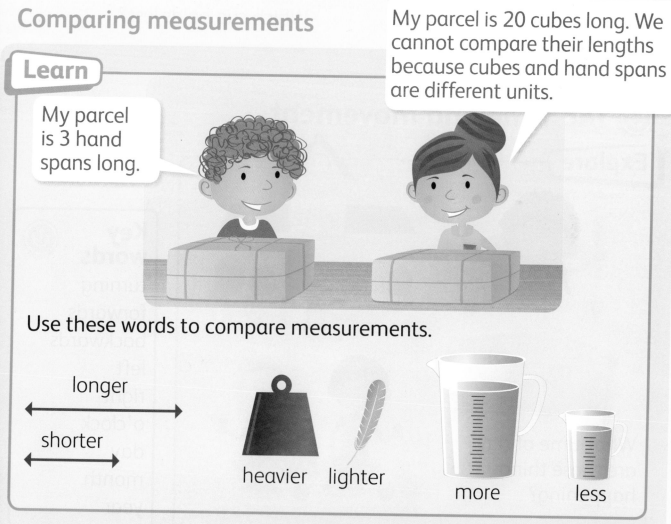

Use these words to compare measurements.

longer

shorter

heavier    lighter

more        less

## Practise

Compare the objects.

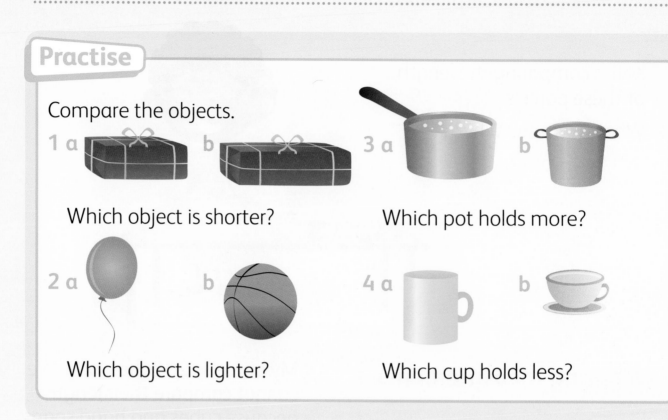

1 a    b

Which object is shorter?

2 a    b

Which object is lighter?

3 a    b

Which pot holds more?

4 a    b

Which cup holds less?

## ⟳ 14c Time and movement

### Explore

What time of day are these things happening?

**Key words** ⟳
turning
forwards
backwards
left
right
o'clock
day
month
year

# ⟳ Months of the year

**Learn**

| January | February | March |
|---------|----------|-------|
| April   | May      | June  |
| July    | August   | September |
| October | November | December |

We can learn the months of the year by using Look, Cover, Say, Check.

**Look** carefully at the months.

**Cover** them up using a piece of paper.

**Say** them in order.

**Check** if you were right.

Do you know all the days of the week in order?

Think of anything special that happens on any of these days.

Use Look, Cover, Say, Check to see if you can remember the days in order.

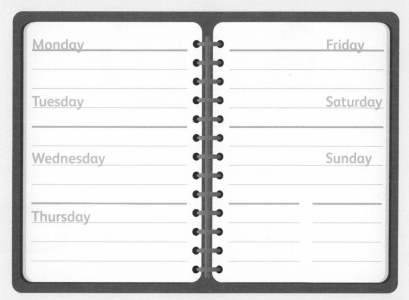

Monday          Friday

Tuesday          Saturday

Wednesday          Sunday

Thursday

Practise

## Practise

1 Olubayo is trying to peg these days of the week cards in order.

  a Say the correct order to help him.

  b Help him with the months of the year too.

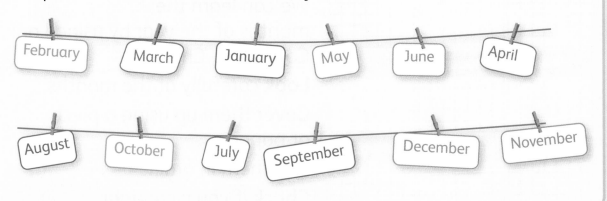

## Moving around

### Learn

Things can move in different ways.

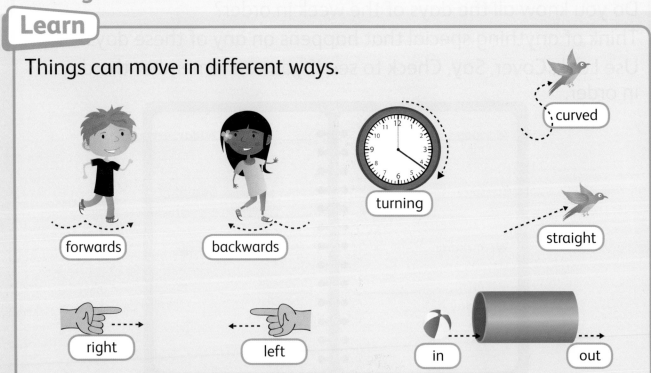

forwards · backwards · turning · curved · straight · right · left · in · out

## Practise

1  Are they moving to the left or the right?

a

b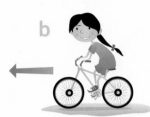

c

 **More o'clock times**

## Learn

There are
24 hours in one day.
Each time a new
hour starts, the
minute hand on a clock reaches
the 12 and makes an o'clock time.

one day

| 1 | 2 | 3 | 4 | 5 | 6 | 7 | 8 | 9 | 10 | 11 | 12 |
|---|---|---|---|---|---|---|---|---|----|----|----|
| 13 | 14 | 15 | 16 | 17 | 18 | 19 | 20 | 21 | 22 | 23 | 24 |

hours

minute hand

hour hand

 The minute hand is pointing straight upwards. This shows us it is an o'clock time.

 The hour hand shows us which o'clock time it is. So it is 7 o'clock.

## Practise

1  Use a clock to make these o'clock times.
   The first one has been done for you.

a  two o'clock

b  six o'clock

c  ten o'clock

d  twelve o'clock

e  four o'clock

The minute hand is pointing to the 12 and the hour hand is pointing to the nine.

The minute hand is pointing to the 12 and the hour hand is pointing to the twelve.

2  What o'clock times do these clocks show?

a

__ o'clock

b

__ o'clock

c

__ o'clock

d  Which time is most likely for learners to be at school?

e  Which time is most likely to be dinner time?

f  Which time is most likely to be when school finishes?

## Self-check

### A Money

**1** Kendrick and Jazzie each have 13 cents.
Kendrick has 4 coins. Jazzie has more than 4 coins.
Use coins to show how both children have 13 cents.
Explain how you made the amounts.

### B Measures

**1**

 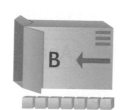 

Box ___ is shorter than Box ___ but longer than Box ___.

**2**

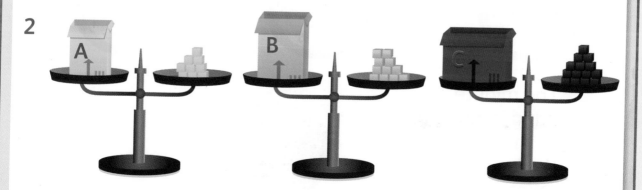

Box ___ is lighter than Box ___ but heavier than Box ___.

**3**

  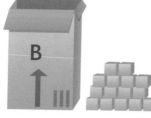  

Box ___ holds less than Box ___ but more than Box ___.

## C Time

**1** Write the missing days of the week. Then put them in the correct order.

( Saturday )  ( ? )  ( Friday )  ( Wednesday )

( ? )  ( Monday )  ( ? )

**2** Write the months of the year in the correct order.

( July ) ( November ) ( May ) ( December ) ( February ) ( October )

( January ) ( March ) ( June ) ( September ) ( April ) ( August )

**3** What o'clock times do these clocks show?

a   b  c

d
The minute hand is pointing to the 12 and the hour hand is pointing to the six.

## ⏻ 15a Problem solving

### Problem 1

Class 1 are visiting the park.

1 What time will the park gates open?

2 The park café closes at three o'clock. What will the hands on the park clock look like at three o'clock?

## Problem 2

The park gardener is planting rows of flowers.

Each row has some yellow and some blue flowers.

Each row has 10 flowers altogether.

Here is one of the rows he has planted:

2 yellow flowers and 8 blue flowers make 10.

**a** Which other pairs of numbers could he use to make 10?

| 10 | |
|---|---|
| 1 + 9 | 6 + ☐ |
| 2 + ☐ | 7 + ☐ |
| 3 + ☐ | 8 + ☐ |
| 4 + ☐ | 9 + ☐ |
| 5 + ☐ | |

**b** Jo looks at the row of flowers and thinks of two number facts:

2 + 8 = 10   and   10 − 2 = 8

Look at this row of flowers.

Can you make one adding fact and one take away fact from it?

## Problem 3

| 1 | 2 | 3 | 4 | 5 | 6 | 7 | 8 | 9 | 10 |
|---|---|---|---|---|---|---|---|---|---|
| 11 | 12 | 13 | 14 | 15 | 16 | 17 | 18 | 19 | 20 |
| 21 | 22 | 23 | 24 | 25 | 26 | 27 | 28 | 29 | 30 |
| 31 | 32 | 33 | 34 | 35 | 36 | 37 | 38 | 39 | 40 |
| 41 | 42 | 43 | 44 | 45 | 46 | 47 | 48 | 49 | 50 |
| 51 | 52 | 53 | 54 | 55 | 56 | 57 | 58 | 59 | 60 |
| 61 | 62 | 63 | 64 | 65 | 66 | 67 | 68 | 69 | 70 |
| 71 | 72 | 73 | 74 | 75 | 76 | 77 | 78 | 79 | 80 |
| 81 | 82 | 83 | 84 | 85 | 86 | 87 | 88 | 89 | 90 |
| 91 | 92 | 93 | 94 | 95 | 96 | 97 | 98 | 99 | 100 |

There is a hundred square painted on the ground.

Suki makes patterns by putting hoops on some of the squares.

Here is what some of her friends say about her pattern:

**A** The hoops are on even numbers.

**B** They are all multiples of 10.

**C** You are counting in twos.

a Which two friends are correct?
Change the wrong statement to make it correct.

b Suki wants to make a new pattern starting on 8 and adding 10 each time. What will her pattern look like?

Will one of her numbers be 27? Why? Why not?

## Problem 4

In the café, Aisha is choosing what to eat.

| | |
|---|---|
| lemonade | **13c** |
| bottled water | **20c** |
| ice cream | **15c** |
| apple | **18c** |

a What can she buy with her money?

b Rupi says: "I have the same amount of money as you. But I have different coins." What coins could Rupi have?

## Problem 5

Lori and Pasha have drawn a circle in the sand pit to make a Venn diagram.

They are using it to sort 2-D shapes.

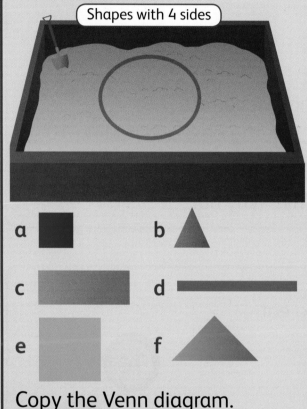

Shapes with 4 sides

a ■    b ▲

c ▬    d ▬

e ■    f ▲

Copy the Venn diagram. Draw the shapes on it.

## Problem 6

Next to a bench, there are 13 crumbs of bread left on the ground.

A bird eats some of them and leaves 8 on the ground.

How many crumbs are left?

## Problem 7

Garcia, Christiano and Alesana are collecting leaves to make a collage.

Garcia has 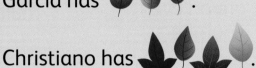.

Christiano has .

Alesana has 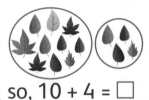.

How many leaves do they have altogether?

We can work out the total quickly if we can find a pair that make 10.

 and

make 10.

so, 10 + 4 = ☐

a Use cubes to show how to do this.

b Three more children collect 5 leaves, 4 leaves and 6 leaves. How many do they have altogether?

# Mathematical dictionary

**2-dimensional (2-D)** a flat shape with sides and angles

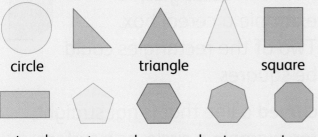

circle    triangle    square

rectangle  pentagon  hexagon  heptagon  octagon

**3-dimensional (3-D)** a solid shape with faces, edges and corners

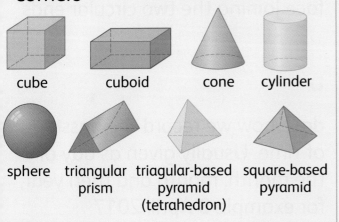

cube    cuboid    cone    cylinder

sphere  triangular prism  triagular-based pyramid (tetrahedron)  square-based pyramid

## A

**add** combine two or more numbers or objects to find a total

**after** following a number or time

**altogether** a collection of numbers or objects; in total

**amount** the number of objects or numbers

## B

**backwards** moving in the direction behind you

**balance** things are balanced when both sides have equal value, for example 3 + 4 = 2 + 5

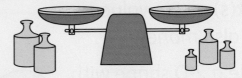

**before** in front of, earlier

**between** in the middle of two other numbers or objects

**bigger** larger in size

**block graph** a diagram that shows information

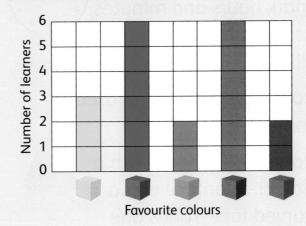

Number of learners

Favourite colours

## C

**calendar** a list of the days of the year, arranged by month, week and day

167

**capacity** the amount a container holds

**Carroll diagram** a table used for grouping things

| Less than 11 | More than 11 |
|---|---|
|  |  |

**cent(s)** a coin value
See also *money*

**circle** a 2-D shape with one curved side and no straight sides

**clock, clock face, hands** a clock is used to show and record time. It can have a circular face with revolving hands to mark hours and minutes, or it can have a digital display

**coin** a piece of metal used as money

**cone** a 3-D shape with a flat, circular face and a curved face. It has one point

**corner** the point on a 2-D shape where two sides meet

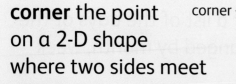
corner →

**cube** a 3-D shape made from six square faces

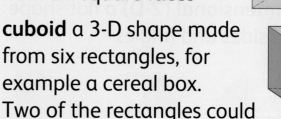

**cuboid** a 3-D shape made from six rectangles, for example a cereal box. Two of the rectangles could be squares

**curved** a line that is not straight, for example a circle, or a surface that is not flat, for example an egg

**cylinder** a 3-D shape with circular ends and one curved face joining the two circular ends

**D**

**date** how we record the passing of time. Usually given as day of the month, month and then year, for example 3 April, 2017

**difference** how much bigger or smaller one quantity is compared to another. Usually found by subtraction:

The difference between 7 and 5 is 2; $7 - 5 = 2$

**different** not the same as another

**digit** the symbols 0, 1, 2, 3, 4, 5, 6, 7, 8 and 9

**double** two lots of something, multiply by 2; twice as many

**E**

**edge** the line made where two faces of a 3-D shape meet. See also *face*

**equals** symbol: (=) means to have the same value as, for example 2 + 4 = 6; 5 + 3 = 7 + 1

**estimate** a sensible guess at how many or how much

**even** a whole number that can be grouped in twos. It is a multiple of 2. All numbers ending in 0, 2, 4, 6 or 8. See also *odd*

**exchange** swap

**F**

**face** a flat surface on a 3-D shape. See also *edge*

**first** before anything or anyone else; the number one in order

**flat** in 2-D and 3-D shapes, not curved

**forwards** moving in the direction you are facing, straight in front of you

**H**

**half** when a whole is divided into two equal parts

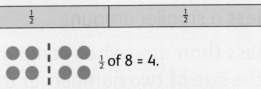

½ of 8 = 4.

**heavier** an object that weighs more than another object

**heavy, light** words used to compare mass or weight

light
heavy

**hexagon** a 2-D shape with six straight sides

**hour** symbol: (h) A measure of time (60 minutes). See also *minute* and *second*

**hour hand** the short hand on a clock that measures the hours. One complete turn takes 12 hours. See also *minute hand*

hour hand

**how many** what number or total

## L

**left** the direction in which this arrow points ←

**length, height** words used to describe how long or tall something is; how far from one point to the other

**less** a smaller amount

**less than** used when comparing the size of two numbers or things, for example 7 is less than 10. See also *more than*

**lighter** an object that weighs less then another object

**longer** more in measurement

**longest** the most in measurement

## M

**measure** to find out the size of something

**minute** symbol: (min) A measure of time, there are 60 minutes in one hour. See also *second* and *hour*

**minute hand** the hand on a clock face that measures the minutes. See also *hour hand*

minute hand

**money** coins and notes used to buy things with

**month** there are 12 months in a year: January, February, March, April, May, June, July, August, September, October, November and December

**more** a bigger amount

**more than** used when comparing the size or total of numbers or things. 10 is more than 7. See also *less than*

**multiple, multiple of** when we start at zero and count in steps of the same size, those numbers are multiples of that step. So 2, 4, 6, 8, 10 are all multiples of 2

## N

**near double** almost twice as many

**number** there are many different types of number, including counting numbers 0, 1, 2, 3 and so on; ordinal numbers 1st, 2nd, 3rd and so on

**number bonds/pairs** an addition fact, for example the number bonds for 10 are all pairs of whole numbers, like 2 and 8, which add up to 10

**number sentence** a sentence of numbers and symbols, for example 6 − 3 = 3

## O

**o'clock** a way of describing an hour time, for example 5 o'clock. The minute hand always points to the 12. See also *half past*

5 o'clock

**odd** all numbers ending in 1, 3, 5, 7 or 9

**one less** the number one whole before that number on a number line, for example 9 is one less than 10

**one more** the next whole number after that number on a number line, for example 9 is one more than 8

**ones** numbers in the ones place of any number, for example 14 is one 10 and 4 ones

**order** put things in their correct place, following a rule

## P

**pair** two of something

**partition** separate a number into different parts

**parts** different pieces that something is made of

**pattern** numbers, shapes or symbols that are repeated and follow a rule

**pentagon** a 2-D shape with five straight sides

**pictogram** a picture that shows a word

**prism** a solid shape with two identical ends and flat sides

**pyramid, square-based** a 3-D shape with a square base and four triangular faces

## R

**rectangle** a 2-D shape with four straight sides. A square is a special sort of rectangle with all four sides the same length.

171

**reflection** something that would be seen in a mirror

**right** the direction in which this arrow points

S

**same** not different, identical

**second** a period of time; there are 60 seconds in a minute

**second** the number two in order

**shape** a 2-D or 3-D object

**sharing** putting objects into equal-sized groups, one at a time

**shorter** not as long as another object

**shortest** measuring a small object or distance from end to end

**side** a position to the left or right of an object; on a 2-D shape, for example a triangle has three sides, a rectangle has 4. See also *corner*

side

side

side

**smaller** of a size less than another object

**sort** to divide shapes with the same rules into different groups

**sphere** a 3-D shape like a ball

**square** a shape with four sides of equal length

**straight line** a straight line has no curves or corners. It can be drawn using a ruler. See also *curved*

**subtract** to take away something from another

**subtraction** a subtraction finds the difference between two numbers. Also called taking away, for example 10 − 3 = 7 (the difference)

**symmetrical** each half is exactly the same

# T

**take away** another name for subtraction. See also *subtraction*

**tall, taller, tallest** words used when comparing two or more heights, for example: Amy is taller than Lili, but Theo is the tallest

**tens** shows the tens place value

**third** the number three in order

**time** a measurement of an action or event

**total** the answer to an addition calculation

**triangle** a 2-D shape with three straight sides

**turning** change direction, for example change from facing forwards to facing left

**twice** two times

# U

**unit** an amount of measurement

# V

**value** how much something is worth

**Venn diagram** a diagram with circles to show sets

# W

**week** there are 7 days in a week: Monday, Tuesday, Wednesday, Thursday, Friday, Saturday and Sunday

**weight** how much something weighs

# Y

**year** 365 (or 366) days make a year

| JANUARY | | | | | | |
|---|---|---|---|---|---|---|
| M | T | W | T | F | S | S |
|  |  |  |  | 1 | 2 | 3 |
| 4 | 5 | 6 | 7 | 8 | 9 | 10 |
| 11 | 12 | 13 | 14 | 15 | 16 | 17 |
| 18 | 19 | 20 | 21 | 22 | 23 | 24 |
| 25 | 26 | 27 | 28 | 29 | 30 | 31 |

| FEBRUARY | | | | | | |
|---|---|---|---|---|---|---|
| M | T | W | T | F | S | S |
| 1 | 2 | 3 | 4 | 5 | 6 | 7 |
| 8 | 9 | 10 | 11 | 12 | 13 | 14 |
| 15 | 16 | 17 | 18 | 19 | 20 | 21 |
| 22 | 23 | 24 | 25 | 26 | 27 | 28 |
| 29 |  |  |  |  |  |  |

| MARCH | | | | | | |
|---|---|---|---|---|---|---|
| M | T | W | T | F | S | S |
|  |  |  |  |  | 5 | 6 |
| 7 | 8 | 9 | 10 | 11 | 12 | 13 |
| 14 | 15 | 16 | 17 | 18 | 19 | 20 |
| 21 | 22 | 23 | 24 | 25 | 26 | 27 |
| 28 | 29 | 30 | 31 |  |  |  |

| APRIL | | | | | | |
|---|---|---|---|---|---|---|
| M | T | W | T | F | S | S |
|  |  |  |  | 1 | 2 | 3 |
| 4 | 5 | 6 | 7 | 8 | 9 | 10 |
| 11 | 12 | 13 | 14 | 15 | 16 | 17 |
| 18 | 19 | 20 | 21 | 22 | 23 | 24 |
| 25 | 26 | 27 | 28 | 29 | 30 |  |

| MAY | | | | | | |
|---|---|---|---|---|---|---|
| M | T | W | T | F | S | S |
|  |  |  |  |  |  | 1 |
| 2 | 3 | 4 | 5 | 6 | 7 | 8 |
| 9 | 10 | 11 | 12 | 13 | 14 | 15 |
| 16 | 17 | 18 | 19 | 20 | 21 | 22 |
| 23/30 | 24/31 | 25 | 26 | 27 | 28 | 29 |

| JUNE | | | | | | |
|---|---|---|---|---|---|---|
| M | T | W | T | F | S | S |
|  |  | 1 | 2 | 3 | 4 | 5 |
| 6 | 7 | 8 | 9 | 10 | 11 | 12 |
| 13 | 14 | 15 | 16 | 17 | 18 | 19 |
| 20 | 21 | 22 | 23 | 24 | 25 | 26 |
| 27 | 28 | 29 | 30 |  |  |  |

| JULY | | | | | | |
|---|---|---|---|---|---|---|
| M | T | W | T | F | S | S |
|  |  |  |  | 1 | 2 | 3 |
| 4 | 5 | 6 | 7 | 8 | 9 | 10 |
| 11 | 12 | 13 | 14 | 15 | 16 | 17 |
| 18 | 19 | 20 | 21 | 22 | 23 | 24 |
| 25 | 26 | 27 | 28 | 29 | 30 | 31 |

| AUGUST | | | | | | |
|---|---|---|---|---|---|---|
| M | T | W | T | F | S | S |
| 1 | 2 | 3 | 4 | 5 | 6 | 7 |
| 8 | 9 | 10 | 11 | 12 | 13 | 14 |
| 15 | 16 | 17 | 18 | 19 | 20 | 21 |
| 22 | 23 | 24 | 25 | 26 | 27 | 28 |
| 29 | 30 | 31 |  |  |  |  |

| SEPTEMBER | | | | | | |
|---|---|---|---|---|---|---|
| M | T | W | T | F | S | S |
|  |  |  | 1 | 2 | 3 | 4 |
| 5 | 6 | 7 | 8 | 9 | 10 | 11 |
| 12 | 13 | 14 | 15 | 16 | 17 | 18 |
| 19 | 20 | 21 | 22 | 23 | 24 | 25 |
| 26 | 27 | 28 | 29 | 30 |  |  |

| OCTOBER | | | | | | |
|---|---|---|---|---|---|---|
| M | T | W | T | F | S | S |
|  |  |  |  |  | 1 | 2 |
| 3 | 4 | 5 | 6 | 7 | 8 | 9 |
| 10 | 11 | 12 | 13 | 14 | 15 | 16 |
| 17 | 18 | 19 | 20 | 21 | 22 | 23 |
| 24/31 | 25 | 26 | 27 | 28 | 29 | 30 |

| NOVEMBER | | | | | | |
|---|---|---|---|---|---|---|
| M | T | W | T | F | S | S |
|  | 1 | 2 | 3 | 4 | 5 | 6 |
| 7 | 8 | 9 | 10 | 11 | 12 | 13 |
| 14 | 15 | 16 | 17 | 18 | 19 | 20 |
| 21 | 22 | 23 | 24 | 25 | 26 | 27 |
| 28 | 29 | 30 |  |  |  |  |

| DECEMBER | | | | | | |
|---|---|---|---|---|---|---|
| M | T | W | T | F | S | S |
|  |  |  | 1 | 2 | 3 | 4 |
| 5 | 6 | 7 | 8 | 9 | 10 | 11 |
| 12 | 13 | 14 | 15 | 16 | 17 | 18 |
| 19 | 20 | 21 | 22 | 23 | 24 | 25 |
| 26 | 27 | 28 | 29 | 30 | 31 |  |

# Resources

Trace over the numbers.

| 1 | 2 | 3 | 4 |
| 5 | 6 | 7 | 8 |
| 9 | 10 | 11 | 12 |
| 13 | 14 | 15 | 16 |
| 17 | 18 | 19 | 20 |

# Number grid

| 1 | 2 | 3 | 4 | 5 | 6 | 7 | 8 | 9 | 10 |
|---|---|---|---|---|---|---|---|---|---|
| 11 | 12 | 13 | 14 | 15 | 16 | 17 | 18 | 19 | 20 |
| 21 | 22 | 23 | 24 | 25 | 26 | 27 | 28 | 29 | 30 |
| 31 | 32 | 33 | 34 | 35 | 36 | 37 | 38 | 39 | 40 |
| 41 | 42 | 43 | 44 | 45 | 46 | 47 | 48 | 49 | 50 |
| 51 | 52 | 53 | 54 | 55 | 56 | 57 | 58 | 59 | 60 |
| 61 | 62 | 63 | 64 | 65 | 66 | 67 | 68 | 69 | 70 |
| 71 | 72 | 73 | 74 | 75 | 76 | 77 | 78 | 79 | 80 |
| 81 | 82 | 83 | 84 | 85 | 86 | 87 | 88 | 89 | 90 |
| 91 | 92 | 93 | 94 | 95 | 96 | 97 | 98 | 99 | 100 |

# Number line

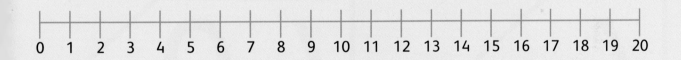

0 1 2 3 4 5 6 7 8 9 10 11 12 13 14 15 16 17 18 19 20

# Tens frames

## Arrow cards

1

2

3

4

5

10

20

30

40

50